The Marketing of the President

*This book is dedicated to my father, Samuel Newman.
Dad, thank you for your love,
support, and wise guidance
throughout my career and life.*

The Marketing of the President
Political Marketing as Campaign Strategy

Bruce I. Newman

SAGE Publications
International Educational and Professional Publisher
Thousand Oaks   London   New Delhi

For information address:

SAGE Publications, Inc.
2455 Teller Road
Thousand Oaks, California 91320

SAGE Publications Ltd.
6 Bonhill Street
London EC2A 4PU
United Kingdom

SAGE Publications India Pvt. Ltd.
M-32 Market
Greater Kailash I
New Delhi 110 048 India

Printed in the United States of America

Library of Congress Cataloging-in-Publication Data

Newman, Bruce I.
    The marketing of the president : political marketing as campaign
strategy / Bruce I. Newman.
        p.   cm.
    Includes bibliographical references and index.
    ISBN 0-8039-5137-X. —   ISBN 0-8039-5138-8 (pbk.)
    1. Presidents—United States—Election. 2. Campaign management—
United States. 3. Electioneering—United States. 4. Marketing—
United States. I. Title.
JK528.N48   1994
324.7'0973—dc20   93-32450
                                                                 CIP

94 95 96 97 98 10 9 8 7 6 5 4 3 2

Sage Production Editor: Rebecca Holland

Contents

Acknowledgments

This book could not have been finished without the help of many individuals. First of all, I want to thank Harry Briggs, Editorial Director of Sage Publications, for giving me his support throughout the project. Harry was a constant source of encouragement, flexible when he needed to be, and always understanding. I truly enjoyed working with him on this project. I also want to thank the staff at Sage, including Marquita Flemming, acquisitions editor; Rebecca Holland, production editor; Yvonne Könneker, copy editor; Stephanie Varnell, promotion manager; and Nancy Hale, editorial assistant. It was truly a pleasure to work with people who displayed the highest level of professionalism at every stage of this project.

Next I would like to thank Dean Ron Patten of the Kellstadt Graduate School of Business for his support and the Office of Sponsored Programs at DePaul University for awarding me a leave of absence, which was used to finish this book. Without the luxury of a leave from full-time teaching duties during the last stages of my work on the book, I could not have finished it in a timely fashion.

There are several people who deserve special mention for their help in the early stages of my thinking for this book. First of all, I want to thank Jagdish Sheth of Emory University for his critique of the final manuscript and for his assistance with the development of some ideas that were used to structure the outline of the book. We have worked together for 20 years now, and our close friendship continues to be a source of energy to me. Both Louis Larrea and Bob Pitts, colleagues of mine at DePaul University, were very instrumental in helping me to refine my ideas in the first stages of the manuscript. Bob and I had several late-night discussions about the direction the book should take at critical junctures in its development.

The final manuscript was reviewed by several individuals, academic and nonacademic, whose comments were crucial to my shaping of the final product. On the academic side, I would like to thank Elaine Sherman of Hofstra University, Leon Schiffman of Baruch College, Joseph Ben-ur of the University of Wisconsin-Milwaukee, and Larry Bennett of DePaul University. Each of these individuals offered a professional insight that helped improve my thinking in many areas of the book. Several reviewers who were not academics offered me insights that exposed my thinking to the interested citizen. I have several people to thank, including Kris Volkman, Henry Davis, Louis Newman, Burton Newman, and Rochelle Rubinoff. Each of their comments was constructive but, at the same time, different. It was amazing to me how each one could read the same manuscript and focus on totally different issues, one as relevant as the other.

A final and special thanks goes to my family—my wife, Judy, my son, Todd, and my daughter, Erica—for putting up with my rigorous work schedule and for putting up with me. Thanks for letting me take precious time away from you to work on my book. Judy, thanks for your patience, love, and constant encouragement.

Foreword

A market-oriented approach to political elections is becoming increasingly inevitable everywhere in the world because of a number of fundamental changes that are occurring today and will continue in the foreseeable future.

Obviously, the collapse of the communist ideology has eliminated communism as a political governance option. The only acceptable alternatives are political anarchy and the threat of civil wars or the embracement of a democratic form of government. Since political anarchy is not in the self-interest of the politicians, it is more likely that a market-oriented approach to getting elected and reelected will be embraced in most emerging democracies.

Another major factor encouraging market orientation in politics is the ubiquitous presence of news and information at any time and anywhere with the advent of radio and television virtually everywhere in the world. The "global village" has made the political election process more democratic and less elitist because you don't have to be literate to make candidate choices. In other words, the old system of party controlled newspapers and magazines catering to the educated elite, especially in the European parliamentary democracy, is no longer sufficient to perpetuate political power. The candidates must appeal more directly to all types of voters as if they were customers in the market place.

A third major force encouraging the market-oriented approach to political elections is the availability and ability of information technology (computers and communications) to target individual voters, literally enabling political campaigns to practice segment of one marketing. This is similar to what other service industries have recently implemented; for example, mail order catalog stores (L.L. Bean), airlines (frequent flyer programs), long distance telephone companies (MCI's "Friends and Family" or AT&T's "I" plan), and others. This database capability allows and encourages political candidates to extend their reach and customize their appeal without being bound by location and time boundaries.

Finally, and perhaps most importantly, the public has become cynical about political parties and political candidates to the extent that *caveat emptor* (buyer beware) is regarded as a safer approach to choosing parties and candidates than relying on the opinions of leaders, the press, party, or other institutions. In other words, the average public believes that they must personally take charge and even become vigilante voters, in the same way they approach such societal problems as public education, crime, and health care.

Perceived risks associated with making wrong political choices are significant today with respect to both performance uncertainty and economic, social, and emotional costs. Building trust and making commitments will become increasingly imperative for political candidates not only to get elected the first time but also to be continually reelected. This was painfully demonstrated in the last election, especially in the House of Congress where a record number of new candidates were voted in, partly because the "old guard" could not sustain public trust.

The Marketing of the President is an exceptional book. It not only points out in a compelling way why market orientation has become inevitable, but it also provides a framework and a step-by-step marketing process with which to develop and execute political campaigns. Its insights into how President Clinton, the "comeback kid," actually practiced the marketing concept to win the national election is reminiscent of the earlier best-seller books that focused on the making of the president (John F. Kennedy) or selling of the president (Richard M. Nixon). Bruce Newman also adds intrigue and suspense by focusing on Ross Perot and his political impact on future elections: Will he be the Wallace of the nineties?

The 1996 presidential election will not be the same for me after reading this book. I will be analyzing each candidate's campaign strategy, style, and context from a marketing perspective!

DR. JAGDISH N. SHETH,
Charles H. Kellstadt
Professor of Marketing,
Emory University

Preface

They called him the "comeback kid," the candidate who catapulted from the back of the pack to become the leader of the free world. That's one way of describing Bill Clinton's miraculous feat of winning the 1992 presidential campaign. Here was a candidate who by all accounts was finished before the race even started. The New Hampshire primary was just heating up when the accusations about Clinton's alleged infidelity hit the news. Then there was the bold move to confront the allegations and go live on *60 Minutes* with his wife, Hillary. As millions of Americans watched the Clintons talk about their private lives that Sunday night, we saw the first glimpse of many shocking events that would highlight this campaign. However, the real story in this election was not about the shocking events, colorful personalities, or unusual manner in which the election campaign was conducted. The real story reveals itself in Clinton's successful use of marketing to win the election: The same tools used to market a wide array of products and services were used to market Bill Clinton. This book elaborates on how these tools were used and why their use made the difference between winning and losing the campaign.

The Marketing of the President offers an inside view of the development of campaign strategy from a marketer's point of view, which is different from the way journalists and the media document this process. Journalistic accounts of the Clinton victory have been well documented in several postelection publications. In particular, the *Newsweek* "Election Special" did an excellent job of discussing some of the new technologies used in modern-day campaigns. We have all read about some of the marketing tools used by the candidates in 1992, such as focus groups, polls, infomercials, and telemarketing. Instead of making reference to isolated uses of these tools, this book presents the so-called big picture by giving a detailed explanation of not only what marketing is but how the use of it turned Bill Clinton from "Slick Willie" into "Mr. President."

In 1992 we saw the first telemarketing campaign, run by Ross Perot. Here was a candidate who broke all of the conventional rules about campaigning and totally circumvented the electoral process. Ross Perot relied on high tech tactics to compete in presidential politics and, in so doing, altered the course of modern presidential campaigns for elections to come. Without running in a single primary, and without the support of a political party, Perot was still able to win 19% of the popular vote.

Political polls continue to be used as the barometers for the power brokers in the process. Candidates, the media, political parties, political action committees, consultants, and the voters themselves have learned to rely on the expertise of the pollster to get a moment's reading on political reality. The electoral process has changed in this country from voter participation through political parties to direct contact with the candidates. Talk show hosts such as Larry King and Phil Donahue became the conduits between the candidates and the voters. Some have referred to this form of politics as "dial-in democracy."

The winning strategy Bill Clinton used in 1992 was different from the one John Kennedy used in 1960, which relied on "backroom" party bosses to help get him elected. In 1992 we had technological innovations that changed political dynamics. Computerized polls gave the candidates instantaneous results from around the country, satellite hookups allowed the candidates to speak to many different local news stations simultaneously, and multimillion-dollar fund-raising campaigns were carried out with the use of toll-free telephone numbers.

The Clinton campaign organization resembled the best-run marketing organizations in this country, such as Proctor & Gamble, McDonald's, Quaker, and others. And as in these finely tuned marketing-driven organizations, Clinton's campaign organizers kept their finger on the pulse of the consumer, the voter. Just as McDonald's uses marketing research to decide where to open up new restaurant locations, Bill Clinton's pollsters used the same technology to determine which states to target with commercials. Just as Quaker uses focus groups to decide which new products to bring to the marketplace, Bill Clinton's researchers used focus groups to decide on how best to communicate their message of change about the economy to the American people.

The first comprehensive account of how marketing was used in a presidential campaign, this book conveys how the American presidential electoral process has been transformed by marketing, who now controls the electoral process, and what impact this has had on elections in this country. To convey this information, I use the 1992 presidential election as a case study. In the discussions that follow, I will explore how modern marketing techniques used in the "commercial marketplace" have been successfully adapted to the "political marketplace."

Framework of the Book

The model presented in Figure 1.1 (see page 12) will be used to structure the topics found in the next chapters. The model summarizes the "New Political Campaign Technology" and illustrates how marketing is used in the modern age of politics. It brings together into one cohesive framework each of the topics I touch on in chapter 1 and explore in greater detail in the remaining chapters.

In Part I, I detail the evolution in marketing and why its role is becoming more important in running a political campaign. Chapter 1 surveys the evolution of marketing in politics and presents a historical and factual account of how marketing as a system has been integrated into the electoral process.

In chapter 2, I establish the logical foundation for discussing the role of marketing in politics and, in so doing, examine how the focus of the candidate has shifted from a party concept to a marketing concept. This shift is reflected in the movement in power from party bosses to consultants. I then go on to explain why there is a need for the marketing concept, how it affects who controls the electoral process, and what the consequences are for using the marketing approach in the political arena.

In chapter 3, the environmental forces that have brought about the marketing-imposed shift in focus of the candidate are explained, especially the influence of these forces on the marketing and political campaigns being waged by the candidates. The forces are broken down into three areas: (a) technological changes that have taken place in politics, (b) structural shifts in the way political campaigns are run, and (c) the shift in influence of the power brokers who control the political and marketing campaigns.

In Part II, the marketing campaign is covered in detail. Chapters 4, 5, and 6 focus on each of the strategic tools that are employed by the candidate and his organization. Chapter 4 covers market segmentation and, as part of this development, an innovative model of voter behavior is reviewed and used as the basis for the segmentation of the market. Chapter 5 examines candidate positioning and chapter 6 reveals the strategic components of the process, which includes the formulation and implementation of a marketing strategy.

Finally, in Part III, chapter 7 is devoted to the future of political marketing and includes a critique of our electoral process and the role of marketing in getting elected to the White House. I will then look ahead to 1996 to discuss some of the issues that I believe will be critical to the success of candidates running in the next presidential election. This chapter ends with an assessment of who stands to gain and lose power among the power brokers in the next election and a strong warning on the consequences of the misuse of marketing in politics.

Author's Note

At the time of publication, Bill Clinton has been in office just over 9 months. In that time, I have had a chance to reflect on how the same marketing techniques that were used to win the White House for Bill Clinton have been used to shape public opinion. For example, Clinton has set up a "war room" to market his economic package that is similar to the nerve center he set up in Little Rock during the campaign. He has announced that he will use a similar approach to market his health care package to the American people. Clinton has relied on focus groups, marketing surveys, electronic town hall meetings, and telemarketing techniques to refine and target his appeals directly to carefully selected segments of voters and key political opinion leaders.

Unfortunately for Clinton, living up to the "image" that was created for him during the campaign has not been easy. The same marketing techniques that won him the presidency have not, so far, guaranteed him high approval ratings.

We have entered a new era in American politics, one that is going to be shaped by technological advances, such as those discussed in this book. Bill Clinton was "marketed" to the American electorate in much the same way as a product or service is marketed to a consumer, and we are seeing the Clinton administration relying on these same tactics to win approval for their programs. Their "marketing warfare" includes repositioning ideas, responding to constantly changing market conditions, and reformulating strategy in communicating their message to the American people.

BRUCE I. NEWMAN, Ph.D.
DePaul University

PART I

The Evolution of Marketing
in Politics

As we look at presidential elections before 1956, we go back to a point in time when politics operated by the principle of grass-roots efforts (or machine politics). Candidates relied on the national party organization to solicit help from local and state party officials to coordinate a volunteer network of support. (We still see this principle driving campaigns at the local and state levels.) In terms of a marketing orientation, campaigns during this time were driven by the forces of distribution (what we in marketing refer to as the person-to-person contact that takes place as a product is transported from the manufacturer to the wholesaler to the retailer to the consumer). Without the benefit of the technology of television, candidates and their representatives relied on personal contact with the voter to get their messages out.

During the election of 1956 we saw the first presidential contender use television to get his message out to the people, Dwight Eisenhower. But, even then, television was not used at the same level of sophistication as in 1960 (the year many believe was the watershed year for television in presidential politics). John F. Kennedy incorporated into his campaign the technological advances in television to help him win the election. During the debates Kennedy made the best use of this medium, looking more relaxed and at ease than Nixon, and was able to convey a successful image that would land him in the White House.

Television brought with it the first opportunities for candidates to begin to develop campaign platforms that revolved around the crafting of political images. Unlike machine politics, which did not enable candidates to electronically craft an image, the ability of candidates to use television as a medium allowed them to formulate campaign platforms that could be "sold" to the American people. Without the benefit of visual aids, it was nearly impossible for candidates to rely on imagery as the basis for campaign strategy development.

Candidates did not see the real influence of marketing until the Madison Avenue experts made their way into the campaign organizations. Joe McGinniss's account of how the 1968 Nixon campaign relied on a sophisticated advertising campaign to win the White House brought to light the real impact that television had on the electoral process. There has been a continued evolution of marketing into politics since that time; the power structure of the campaign organization has shifted farther away from party bosses, but beyond advertising executives, to a whole new cadre of consultants with marketing expertise. Although I will detail what takes place at the presidential level, the analysis is applicable to elections at the local and state levels insofar as it provides a working framework to understand the role of marketing in political campaigns.

In Part I, I provide the foundation on which to build the argument that the electoral process in this country is being transformed by marketing. In the discussion of this transformation, I focus on three subjects. Chapter 1 defines marketing and presents a framework that explains how marketing is used as a campaign strategy. I then discuss how the same strategic tools used to market products and services could be successfully adapted to Bill Clinton's 1992 political campaign. Chapter 2 presents a historical background of the evolution of marketing in politics, with an explanation behind why marketing has become so critical to the success of candidates in the last several presidential elections. The shift in power from the party bosses to the consultants will be analyzed in detail. Finally, in chapter 3, I outline the forces that brought about this change in campaigning. I define who the power brokers are, both old and new, and how the 1992 presidential campaign changed the power structure among these participants.

★ 1 ★

The New Political Campaign Technology

The 1992 presidential election was unique in that it went directly to the people and, in the process of doing so, used the most sophisticated marketing techniques found in the commercial marketplace. We have all heard about direct mail and have certainly seen it pile up in our mailboxes. This same technology used to target direct mail to residences was used to target fund-raising letters to voters of various political persuasions; similarly, techniques used to market products in the mail directly to us as consumers were used to market the candidates us to us as voters.

This was the year of the outsider, which, perhaps more than any other element in the campaign, set the stage for the winning theme, namely, "change." The American voter was tired of politics as usual, and there was a great desire for change, particularly in the way presidential campaigns were run. The heavy reliance on negative advertising in 1988 was repudiated in 1992. Voters wanted more direct access to the candidates, and they wanted the debate to revolve around issues and not personalities. And the candidates gave them what they wanted.

The changing participation in the political process was in response to a new kind of political campaign waged in 1992. Voters became more involved and interested in the presidential election as evidenced by the higher turnout. For some candidates, the infomercial supplemented the commercial. We even saw one candidate talk about issues with charts, graphs, and "voodoo sticks."

What really distinguished this campaign from others was the proficiency and mastery with which the Clinton organization was able to follow the marketing concept (namely, that a marketer must first understand the customer's needs and then develop a product that meets those needs). In this case, Clinton campaign staff understood that people wanted change and were most concerned about the economy (more specifically, jobs). Clinton staff grew to understand the people's concerns and consequently hammered home the themes of change and the economy after their convention.

In addition, the Clinton organization was able to take the best ideas from the challengers as they dropped out of the race and implement those ideas in their own rhetoric, demonstrating a competitive orientation that is practiced in the commercial marketplace. The flexibility and adaptability that one would find in the best-run corporations were found in the Clinton organization. Clinton was constantly integrating and updating his campaign to satisfy voter wants and desires in the same efficient and effective manner as Toyota, who did this for years in the automobile industry.

Anyone running for the presidency of the United States must espouse a political philosophy that represents a vision for the future of the country and the world. In 1992 this philosophy was shaped by the use of sophisticated marketing tools that went beyond the use of polls. Political leadership today is driven not only by political ideology but also by marketing. We need to understand that it is not only the polls but marketing that is driving the political process today. Marketing has become an integral part of the development of campaign strategy.[1]

Bill Clinton was marketed to the American people in much the same way that a doctor's or a lawyer's services are marketed to consumers. Clinton's top strategist, James Carville, used the economy and the impact it was having on the middle class as the focus of their campaign strategy. Clinton attacked the last 12 years of Republican government for its poor treatment of the middle class. Clinton saw that the middle class was distressed and promised he would tax the rich who rode the wave of financial success in the 1980s. Clinton was able to effectively communicate the message that the middle class was hurting, needed change and jobs, and that Clinton was the man to do it.

Voters during the 1992 campaign were deeply interested in this election. As in elections prior to this, economics was the driving force; voters were interested because they felt it in their pocketbooks. With cable television viewership increasing since the last election, voters were able to watch their candidates come through direct to them on a whole host of cable television programs.

The viewership found it refreshing to see the candidates on shows other than the usual interview programs we had grown used to. Some say Bill Clinton turned around his stalled campaign by appearing on *The Arsenio Hall Show*, dressed up in funky clothes, wearing dark sunglasses, and playing his saxophone to a cheering audience. We all had to pinch ourselves to believe what we were seeing: Here was a candidate running for the highest office in the land appearing on late-night television, looking more like a pop star than a presidential candidate. Both Bill Clinton and Ross Perot were quick to understand the importance and power of this medium, however, and engaged in it before George Bush did. George Bush, on the other hand, was very cautious and only belatedly worked his way into cable programming after he was trailing badly in the polls.

The question is, why all these appearances on live call-in shows? Some say it was due to the appetite of voters who wanted to feel empowered and in touch with a cast of actors usually not seen in person by most Americans in their lifetimes. In 1992 cable reached into more than 60% of television households. On top of that, the three major networks were losing their audience, something that had been happening for close to ten years. Clinton used televised town meeting formats in almost every primary state, honing skills that would serve him well in the October presidential debates. Larry King (the popular talk show host on CNN) may have started this movement of turning politicians into celebrities that swept the political landscape in 1992.[2]

Another explanation behind the extensive use of live call-in shows was the willingness on the part of Clinton to take the risk of appearing in front of live audiences in an effort to reach voters. As the New Hampshire primary date approached, Clinton found his message about the economy obstructed with the allegations against his personal character. Some have argued that he chose unorthodox and alternative media outlets to recast and promote his perspective. Bush, on the other hand, had all the coverage he wanted as a sitting president.

Structural changes in the political process continued to force candidates to rely on consultants. Federal regulations limiting the contributions of individuals to candidates placed more pressure on direct mail and fund-raising specialists to bring in the dollars necessary to run their campaigns. Today, candidates no longer have the luxury of counting on wealthy contributors to finance their campaigns. Couple this with the less-influential role of the political party and we have the seeds for the new electoral system that has evolved in this country.

The 1992 presidential election has shown us how Clinton was successfully marketed, how Bush was unsuccessfully marketed, and why Perot, a great salesman, could not rely on those skills alone in a market dominated by handlers and experts who know the difference between marketing and selling. In the remainder of this chapter, I will formally introduce the topic of marketing, define it, explain how it plays a role in politics, and explain why this "new political campaign technology" is changing the way the electoral process operates in this country.

So What Is Marketing?

Part of the difficulty of understanding how marketing and politics, two seemingly disparate areas, have merged stems from a misunderstanding of what marketing is. Simply put, marketing is an exchange process. The process centers on a seller (the business) who is exchanging a product or service for money from a buyer (the consumer). The exchange is implemented by the seller through the use of a marketing strategy. A marketing strategy is made up of four components: (a) the product (or service), (b) the development of a promotional campaign, (c) pricing, and (d) distribution (the movement of the good from the manufacturer to the consumer).

In more technical terms, marketing is a needs assessment approach to product innovation that relies on information from the marketplace to help guide research and development. This means that the most successful products are molded around the findings from market research studies. Automobiles and gym shoes are just a few examples of product categories that follow a marketing orientation. The development of new car models and innovative gym shoes, such as the pumps, was based on research findings.

Some people have likewise referred to a candidate as a bar of soap, sug-gesting that a candidate is marketed like a product. This, however, is a myth that has circulated in the popular press for some time now; rather, the candi-date is a service provider and necessarily marketed accordingly. The first reference to a candidate as a product came from the media people who were brought into campaign organizations to develop promotional campaigns. These people came from the business world and directly applied their knowledge of product advertising to candidate advertising. As this association developed, it became commonplace to refer to candidates as products.

However, the candidate is in reality a service provider and offers a service to his consumers, the voters, much in the same way that an insurance agent offers a service to his consumers. In this case, the insurance policy becomes the product sold by the agent. Although I will make references to the marketing of candidates as products throughout the book, it should be kept in mind that the product I am referring to is the campaign platform. To convey the impression that the marketing of candidates is similar to the marketing of a bar of soap is to oversimplify and minimize the uniqueness of the marketing application to politics.

First of all, consumers of soap do not spend nearly as much time and effort in the decision to buy one brand over another as a voter does when deciding to cast a ballot for a candidate. As a result, a buyer of soap will be less involved in the acquisition of information than a voter is. Second, by taking note that a candidate is really a service provider, the distinction between campaigning and governing becomes clearer. The actual delivery of a service that a candidate offers to the voter does not occur until he begins to govern. I have emphasized the point earlier that this book is about the application of marketing to campaigning, not governing, although Clinton returns to some of his mar-keting techniques in his presidency.

Finally, candidates operate in a dynamic environment, fast, changing, and full of obstacles that present marketing challenges that require flexibility. Like corporations around the world that alter their services to respond to a more demanding consumer in the commercial marketplace, candidates have to respond to the fast-paced changes that take place in the political market-place. For example, IBM is working to build up its market share by offering more services to its customers. Companies like IBM have to respond to forces in the environment to be successful; likewise for candidates throughout the political campaign and then in office, as well.

Service marketing incorporates a whole host of strategic issues that are not applicable in the marketing of products because services have unique characteristics that products don't have. Services are intangible (they cannot be seen, felt, or heard before they are consumed), variable (depending on the service provider, the quality of the service can vary), perishable (they cannot be stored like products), and they are inseparable (meaning you can't separate the service from the provider of it). The implication of these differences makes the application of marketing to politics very distinctive, but still very comparable to product marketing.

When applying marketing to politics, the exchange process centers on a candidate who offers political leadership in exchange for a vote from the citizen. The product in politics is the campaign platform, and marketing would require that research and polling be done to help shape the platform of the candidate. In addition, the same research techniques are used to craft an image for the candidate. More than the platform itself, the image, or impression, is what the candidate leaves in the mind of the voter. An image is created by the use of visual impressions that are communicated by the candidate's physical presence, media appearances, and experiences and record as a political leader. Once the candidate gets into office, the other characteristics of services (variability, perishability, and inseparability) become more pertinent to the discussion.

There are, however, three glaring differences between marketing and politics. First of all, there are differences of philosophy. In business the goal is to make a profit, whereas in politics the goal is the successful operation of democracy (at least in this country). Second, winning in politics is sometimes based on a few percentage points, whereas in business the difference between winning and losing is based on huge variations. And third, business often follows through with the implementation of actions based on marketing research results if the business stands to profit, whereas in politics the candidate's own political philosophy often shapes the extent to which marketing research results are followed. That is, although a marketing research study may suggest that a politician advocate a specific view of an issue or policy in order to increase the likelihood of election, the candidate may decide not to follow the suggestion because of philosophical differences.[3]

The differences between marketing and politics have not prevented the practitioners in both areas from working to merge the two. As a result, there are strong similarities between the two disciplines. Both rely on the use of standard marketing tools and strategies, such as marketing research, market segmentation, targeting, positioning, strategy development, and implementation. The voter can be analyzed as a consumer in the political marketplace using the same models and theories in marketing that are used to study consumers in the commercial marketplace. And both are dealing in competitive marketplaces and, as such, need to rely on similar approaches to winning (but each may have several distinct options).[4]

A Model of Political Marketing

The merging of marketing and politics is shown in Figure 1.1. Here I bring together into a single framework the two campaigns: the marketing campaign and the political campaign. The marketing campaign is the heart of the model because it contains the marketing tools that are used to get the candidate successfully through the stages of the political campaign. There are three parts to the marketing campaign: market (voter) segmentation, candidate positioning, and strategy formulation and implementation.

Market segmentation is a process in which all voters are broken down into segments, or groupings, that the candidate then targets with his message. For example, Bill Clinton realized early on in the campaign that one very large market segment, the middle class, was ripe for targeting. The critical decision was finding the right message with which to appeal to this segment. Given the economic problems facing the country, Clinton decided to use various economic appeals, such as the promise of more jobs and better wages. Likewise, the baby boomers were another important market segment identified by the Clinton campaign, and various appeals were targeted directly to this segment. As will be discussed later in the book, the segments that are targeted change as the political campaign moves from one stage to another.

Once the multiple voter segments have been identified, the candidate goes through a process called *candidate positioning*. Positioning is a multistage process that begins with the candidate assessing both his own and his opponents' strengths and weaknesses. For example, Bill Clinton was aware that as a Democrat and an outsider to Washington he was in a good position to criticize the system that Reagan and Bush had governed for close to 12 years. Then the issue of targeting is addressed, in which specific segments are chosen as targets of direct campaign messages. There are several strategic issues that arise in the decision to target one segment as opposed to another.

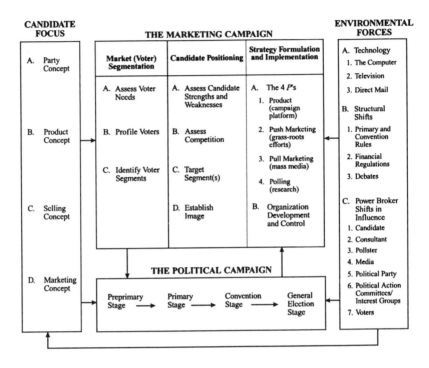

Figure 1.1. A Model of Political Marketing

NOTE: The model integrates four components into a single framework, which will be used to explain how presidential candidates are marketed.

These issues will be fully addressed later in the book, with specific focus on how the Clinton organization successfully carried out its critical targeting task.

What evolves out of this process is the establishment of an image for the candidate. The image is crafted through the media by emphasizing certain personality traits of the candidate, as well as stressing various issues. For example, Bill Clinton created an image of himself as an outsider who would bring about change in Washington through a series of innovative economic programs. From a competitive point of view, he was contending with an incumbent president who was sitting on an economy in recession and not getting results from his actions. Clinton thus capitalized on his strengths and took advantage of his competitors' weaknesses. There were also several other factors attributable to his image as a strong leader that played out during the course of the political campaign. The outcome of this process is the development of a "position" for the candidate.

Once the candidate's position is established, a marketing strategy is developed and implemented. Here, I will explain the "four *P*s," namely, the components in a marketing strategy that are used to reinforce the chosen position of the candidate. The four *P*s include the product, push marketing, pull marketing, and polling. As discussed at length in the previous section, the *product* in politics is the campaign platform. To be successful, a candidate has to market not only himself but his campaign platform as well.

The campaign platform evolves over the course of the political campaign. It is influenced by several factors, including the candidate himself, the people in his organization, the party, and, especially, the voters. After the campaign platform is developed, there are two information channels through which the candidate can promote himself. One channel is labeled *push marketing,* and the second is labeled *pull marketing.* Push marketing is synonymous with the distribution concept previously discussed. That is, the candidate's message about his political platform is communicated (or transferred) from the candidate to campaign workers before it gets to the voter, who is the consumer. One way of getting the message out is through traditional grass-roots efforts, or local and state party mechanisms. In addition, the candidate must rely on these same people to get the vote out on election day; in the primaries and the general election, it is imperative that a candidate have an effective volunteer network to win. A candidate relies on his consultants to coordinate local and state efforts with the national party leaders.

Pull marketing is the second information channel and focuses on the use of the mass media to get the candidate's message out to the voters. There are several options available to a candidate, including television, radio, newspapers, and other media. The 1992 election was unique in that the candidates relied on very unorthodox promotional vehicles (in addition to the more traditional ones) to convey their information. In a word, the candidates took a more direct route to the voter in this election and, in doing so, bypassed traditional media outlets. This meant that candidates spent less time on network news programs and more time on cable programs. There will be more to say about this later in the book.

The last *P* is *polling,* which is conducted throughout the political process to provide the candidate with the information necessary to develop the marketing campaign. In politics, as in marketing, there are many tools and devices that are used to conduct the research. Perhaps the most popular and important one in politics is the poll.

This discussion of strategy ends by covering the organizational issues, including the choice of people, setting up a task chart, monitoring activities, and the crucial role of fund-raising. Similar to the business world, political campaign organizations rely on the same fundamental principles to run their operations. Once the marketing strategy has been developed, the important issue is implementation. One of Clinton's greatest strengths as a candidate was his ability to set up an organization that could successfully implement and communicate his vision for the country to the voters.

The marketing campaign is conducted simultaneously with the political campaign and serves to help the candidate get through each of the four stages— preprimary, primary, convention, and general election—successfully. Both the marketing and the political campaigns are influenced by the candidate's strategic orientation (or what I call his "focus") and by forces in the environment. The candidate's focus has changed along with the evolution of marketing practice in politics, that is, with the progression from a "party concept" to a "marketing concept." This discussion will shed light on the theoretical connection between marketing and politics and will show how the candidate has re-oriented his focus from pleasing party bosses to satisfying voter needs.

The second influence on the two campaigns is environmental. Each force represents an area in which there have been dynamic changes taking place over the last few decades that account for the increasingly important role of marketing in the electoral process. For example, the computer has afforded tremendous technological advances in polling and fund-raising. Structural changes in the primary system have further pressured candidates to rely on marketing experts. For example, candidates depend to a great extent on mass media outlets when they attempt to reach the voters in several different states simultaneously on Super Tuesday. Also, the Federal Election Reform Acts (limiting individual contributions to candidates) have forced candidates to call on the expertise of direct mail specialists to bring in the necessary dollars to run their campaigns.

Finally, there have been tremendous shifts in power among the people who have an influence on politics, namely, the power brokers. The party bosses have seen their power diminish, while the media, pollsters, consultants, political action committees, and voters (in this campaign) have seen their power and influence grow in importance.

A Shift in Power From Party Bosses to Consultants

Consultants received a significant amount of attention in the 1992 presidential election, for a couple of reasons. Not only have they taken over as the new party bosses in politics, resulting in a radical shift in power, but they are recruited and sought out like superstar actors for a high-budget film. In fact, candidates are often not taken seriously until they have brought on board some big-name consultants.

There has been quite a change in the presidential election process since Kennedy's day, when the local political bosses ran the show. In contrast to that time, we witnessed Bill Clinton, who ran as the Washington outsider, divorce himself from the powers that be in Washington. Naturally, as the primaries ebbed and flowed, so did the Washington insiders' feelings toward Clinton. Clinton was at first disowned when he began to look, early on in the campaign, like he was carrying too much baggage to be the front-runner. However, as time went on, the Democratic party had no choice but to embrace Clinton to ensure that there would be a unified party. This was the Democrats' first chance at the White House in 12 years, and the party leaders knew by the time Clinton won Illinois that they had nowhere to turn but to him.[5]

The Role of Negative Advertising

Although nowhere as aggressive as in 1988, there still was negative advertising in 1992. On the positive side, Bush emphasized family, jobs, and peace, while Clinton emphasized the importance of reinvigorating the American dream. Clinton pointed out that it was time for a change from the greed and paralysis of the 1980s. However, both of the candidates relied on negative advertising at times to achieve their goals. Bush's attack was based on three overall appeals that painted a picture of Clinton as a waffler: He attacked Clinton's record in Arkansas, tried to portray Clinton as a fast-talking salesman, and emphasized Clinton's inexperience in foreign affairs. Likewise, Clinton's strategy relied on three major appeals: He focused on Bush's lack of vision for a next term and his desire to stay with the status quo, argued that Bush was out of touch with ordinary Americans, and attacked Bush's foreign policy as too timid, especially in the former Soviet Union.[6]

Part of Bush's problem was that some of the negative advertising was directed at him from someone in his own party, namely, Patrick J. Buchanan, who attacked Bush for not advocating stronger Christian values.[7] But Bush, in his turn, waged a negative campaign against Perot; he accused Perot of hiring private investigators to seek damaging information about him when he was vice president and to cast shadows on his children. Bush portrayed Perot as a candidate who strayed outside the rules that everyone else had to follow. Perot's response to this was a declaration that this was part of the Republicans' dirty tricks. Bush also tried to paint Clinton's trip to the Soviet Union while he was a Rhodes Scholar as a meeting with the Communists. This attack, however, eventually backfired in Bush's face.[8]

The strategy and tactics that Clinton used to fend off Bush's attacks and to shape many of his own were plotted in what James Carville referred to as their "war room." The attacks on Bush were personal in that they referred to Bush as a man who had evaded the responsibilities of his actions. Bush was described as a man who was the willing tool of the wealthy and powerful and whose time in office had caused Americans shame; he literally was depicted as a president who had mishandled virtually every aspect of his presidency. However, the Clinton camp was careful to connect their attacks to Bush's public record.[9] Clinton also attacked Ross Perot by portraying him as a candidate who would soon pass from notice as voters realized how little he could accomplish if he were to win the race.[10]

Innovative in the use of negative advertising in 1992 was the tailoring of attacks to fit specific states and regions; in effect, candidates relied on a more targeted approach to their promotional strategy. Another innovation was the increased number of locally aired commercials (especially on cable stations), as opposed to targeting national markets. One Republican strategist estimated that as much as half of the TV ad budgets ended up in nonnational outlets, whereas in 1980 only 10% did.[11]

All three candidates used private investigators to obtain material to put into their advertisements. Their activities (officially called "opposition research") included looking up any piece of information that could be used to the disadvantage of the opposition. In fact, the Republican party installed a sophisticated computer that instantaneously digested and retrieved information, from the content of Clinton's school yearbooks to every article written about him in Arkansas newspapers. In addition, there was a videotape file that included tapes of every television appearance Clinton had made. It was from a similar archive that James P. Pinkerton, an aid to Bush in the 1988 campaign, found a debate transcript during the primaries in which there was mention of Mr. Dukakis's furlough of Willie Horton (which became one of the more infamous commercials of the 1988 campaign). There are, however, certain unwritten rules that are followed in negative advertising: Avoid using inaccurate information, stay away from sex and drugs, and do not lie about one's identity when obtaining information, but, at the same time, do not go out of the way to identify oneself either.[12]

A Historical Perspective on the Merging of Marketing and Politics

There are several reasons behind the merging of politics and marketing. Perhaps the single most influencial factor has been the use of television and the necessity of candidates to rely on experts in the field of marketing and related areas to help them master this medium. The televised debates that took place during the Kennedy and Nixon campaign in 1960 increased the pressure on candidates to turn to Madison Avenue experts to craft the "correct" image for the electorate. Candidates who are not telegenic and relaxed in front of a camera find it increasingly difficult to win the presidency today.

The Simulmatics project in 1960 was the beginning of another dimension to marketing, namely marketing research, which opened up to politicians a whole new world of numbers and computers that would forever change the course of events in electioneering. At the fingertips of computer and statistical experts was the ability to break down a whole country into regions and localities, which would reveal differences in demographic and socioeconomic makeup as well as in attitudes toward different issues in the campaign.[13]

If we look back at the Carter presidency, we see the use of a sophisticated marketing approach to campaigning and the ability of Carter, with the aid of Pat Caddell, to appeal to multiple voter groups (or segments of consumers). The emphasis in the 1976 presidential election was on personal character and integrity of the two candidates and how little each owed party leaders for their respective candidacies. It was also a year that earmarked a change in political advertising. Leading up to this election since 1964, there was a growth in the use of carefully crafted ads in which the candidates themselves did not make an appearance or speak. However, ironically, in the 1976 campaign, both Jimmy Carter and Gerald Ford returned to the old-fashioned, personal appeals, and personal testimonies re-emerged.[14]

In 1980 we saw another significant change toward the marketing approach campaign when the Republican party chose a candidate, Ronald Reagan, who had decades of experience working in front of the camera and knew how to use the medium to his advantage. In fact, this was never more obvious than when he ran against Walter Mondale, who in contrast looked stiff and ill at ease in front of a camera. In addition to Reagan's good camera persona, his campaign organization represented a well-oiled marketing machine that relied on simple themes, such as patriotism and family, to convey a single and consistent image at every campaign stop and in every commercial. This was accomplished partly by always having hundreds of young flag-waving citizens standing behind Reagan.

The Reagan presidency marked the real beginning of the use of several marketing tools, including negative advertising, direct mail, and sophisticated marketing research and polling as well as the planning and implementation of campaign strategy that closely mirrored what business was doing in the commercial marketplace. In addition to the aid of professional advertising people, Reagan utilized the help of a pollster Richard Wirthlin, who more than any other pollster up to that time understood the significance of running a presidential campaign on the basis of information generated from focus groups and nationwide polls. In fact, Wirthlin was integral in the meaningful leap from the use of polling to marketing research, which essentially meant not only using statistical analysis to predict future voting behavior and to get a snapshot description of who this includes but also getting at voters' underlying motivations.

We also saw the rising influence of political action committees with the Reagan era. Through the use of fund-raising by private sources, Reagan effectively doubled the amount that he was legally permitted to spend. Well-organized groups that opposed social welfare programs spent heavily on television advertising in an effort to get more voters who supported these groups registered.[15]

The 1984 campaign was a study in the power of rhetoric and incumbency as a way of preempting the Democratic challenges in any area where the Republicans may have been vulnerable. The Reagan organization used every asset of incumbency to ensure that none of the Democratic issues would stick. The Reagan ads paraded backdrops with flags raised, houses built, and autos bought, along with a song asserting, "I'm proud to be an American, where at least I know I'm free." On the other hand, the Democrats tried unsuccessfully to create a feeling of discomfort about the budget deficit, the influence of the religious right, the absence of arms control talks with the Soviets, and the financial straits of Americans who had not done well under Reagan.[16]

Mondale was blamed for the Democrats' defeat. He was seen as a dull campaigner and a poor performer on television, plagued by an inefficient campaign organization, and hurt by incoherent advertising. In a nutshell, the problem for the Democrats was not the message but the messenger. Reagan, on the other hand, used both issues and personality to his advantage, with the aid of advertising specialists. In foreign policy, Reagan cited the successful American intervention in Grenada and increased military capability as proof that America had recaptured its standing in the world. The success of Reagan in this election was mainly due to an image that was well crafted for him by his handlers. His image was that of a likable person who successfully combined a confident personality, excellent communication skills, and a strong commitment to religion and family.[17]

The Reagan re-election campaign organization of 1984 continued to use the talents of sophisticated marketing experts in their packaging of Reagan by relying on simple themes of patriotism and family. Again, there was the extensive use of negative advertising. This particular election also represented old versus new politics in that Reagan operated on the basis of the marketing concept, whereas Mondale operated on the basis of a party concept, continuing to rely on old themes and old Democratic grass-roots politics.

In the 1988 presidential election, the Republicans created images that effectively undermined the Democrats' claim to be the party of caring and compassion through the use of the Willie Horton ad, which drove up Dukakis's negatives or, in other words, highlighted his shortcomings. The Republicans turned the slogan Dukakis had used in the primaries against him by altering their attacks to a single focus, namely, risk. The Willie Horton ad ended with the words, "Dukakis wants to do more for America than what he's done for Massachusetts. America can't afford that risk." Dukakis's slogans, on the other hand, shifted from week to week. His ads closed with the claim "They'd like to sell you a package. Wouldn't you rather choose a president?" Slogans from some of Dukakis's more constructive ads included "Let's take charge of America's future," which then turned into "The best America is yet to come." [18]

The success of the Bush campaign was that they attacked early on and consistently and, at the same time, controlled the media and the issue agenda from the convention through election day. When compared with Dukakis's,

Bush's ads were very consistent and tied in well to his debate performance. Dukakis spent much of the campaign trying to counterargue Bush's claims, evidence that Bush was successful in setting the agenda and raising the Dukakis negatives. In 1988 Lee Greenwood's song, "I'm Proud to Be an American" served as an emotional backdrop to the highly charged, flag-filled scenes that made up the Bush election campaign.

Segments from the 1984 *Morning in America* ads were included in the Bush convention film and election eve program. In addition, other ads played on the 1984 themes, such as recapturing the small-town atmosphere in America. Bush dominated the positive side of television air time, playing the role of the parent and grandparent, lifting one of his grandchildren into the air, and preparing a meal in a large kettle, surrounded by the other Bush grandchildren picnicking on the lawn. The Republicans took over from the Democrats their traditional reputation as the party of caring and compassion. In addition, Bush's use of fear was as sophisticated as any since Johnson's use of the daisy in the 1964 campaign.[19]

Marketing and the 1992 Presidential Election

It was truly a new era in politics in 1992, with candidates appearing on late-night television programs dominated by celebrities. No longer could candidates rely on the right backdrop and getting onto the evening news to win. This was a different kind of election, one that has started a new type of campaigning never seen before. Candidates circumvented the traditional communication links with voters and made direct contact through live talk shows. Ross Perot even announced his candidacy on the *Larry King Live* show.

The focus group concept became the newest tool to be adopted by the media during the 1992 election. For example, it was not uncommon to see television journalists conducting live focus groups immediately after the debates as a way of analyzing the performance of the candidates. Polls continued to be heavily relied on by all of the power brokers. Hardly a news broadcast during the election went by without the latest results being reported from a poll. These tools overdramatized every speech a candidate made to the point of creating a horse-race mentality in the election.

In 1992 we saw the first telemarketing campaign run by Ross Perot, a candidate who refused to let the media shape him and instead helped shape the media. Instead of making campaign appearances like most presidential candidates do, this candidate relied on television commercials, videocassettes sent directly to voters, and infomercials to get his message out. In addition, he incorporated some of the latest advances in the direct-marketing area (referred to as database marketing in the commercial marketplace), using an "800" number to solicit a volunteer network and campaign contributions to his organization.

Furthermore, in this campaign issues were discussed more substantively than they were in the 1988 campaign. Modern-day presidential elections are increasingly becoming marketing campaigns. Although modern-day campaigning is not studied as seriously by marketing academics as it is by political scientists and other social scientists, the fact remains that elections today are run by a combination of experts both practicing and theorizing about the influence of marketing on politics.

Conclusion

It has been 24 years since Joe McGinniss wrote his book, *The Selling of the President*, captivating the American public with his account of the role of media in presidential campaigns.[20] Since that time, however, we have come a long way in understanding the subtleties of how political campaigns operate. Political campaigns are now centered on the voter, meaning that the candidate must define himself in the voters' eyes in a way that is consistent with their thinking. The challenge to the candidate becomes one of structuring an image consistent with focus group results and tracking polls. This image is then built up around the events of the campaign, which at times can break loose from the control of the handlers and the way they want the candidate's image to be defined.

Views differ about the impact a campaign built around the voter as a consumer will have on the political process. Some argue that viewing the voter as a consumer dilutes the real purpose of the electoral process; it does not allow for a candidate to create a vision for the country but simply means that the candidate says and does whatever is necessary to get elected. In fact, many accused George Bush of saying and doing just that in both of his bids for the White House.

Perhaps the most important question to ask here is whether or not it is conceivable for a candidate *not* to take a marketing perspective as a candidate in the modern age of politics. Clearly the most successful corporations in the world are consumer driven, such as McDonald's, GE, Toyota, and others. In the last few elections won by Reagan and Bush, marketing has been the engine that drove the organization, with the focus centered on the voter. As I will discuss in more detail later in the book, there have been changes taking place in the political environment that have pushed candidates into the laps of the consultants, who fully understand the significance of this orientation.

Once the candidate gets elected, the next agenda is how to use marketing to keep the candidate on top in the polls, get the candidate's policies enacted, and, eventually, get the candidate re-elected. In other words, the same marketing tools that were used to get Clinton into the White House could also be used to govern. Not even one month into his term, for example, Clinton had to call back his top strategist, James Carville, to deal with public opinion problems plaguing him as a result of "nannygate," a problem labeled as such in the media as a result of Clinton's inability to find an attorney general designate who did not have problems with paying taxes for household workers. Two months after this episode, the same team went to work to put together a marketing campaign to ensure that Clinton's economic package passed in Congress.

In the commercial marketplace, when consumers become the focus of a company, efforts are made to bring them better service and value. Companies maintain this orientation to stay competitive. Likewise, a similar trend is expected in politics as the focus of attention becomes centered on the voter. As this happens, the political process stands to be strengthened because candidates will need to direct more attention to concerns of the voters to keep them satisfied. However, if candidates get elected on the basis of promises that are not delivered to the voter once they get into office, then the political process suffers.

Notes

1. Newman & Sheth (1985), p. ix.
2. *Chicago Tribune* (1992, November 1).
3. Kotler (1982), pp. 461-469.
4. Kotler (1982), pp. 461-469.
5. *New York Times* (1992, March 31).
6. *U.S. News and World Report* (1992, March 30), p. 36.
7. *New York Times* (1992, February 28).
8. *New York Times* (1992, June 27).
9. *New York Times* (1992, August 11).

10. *New York Times* (1992, June 10).
11. *U.S. News and World Report* (1992, October 5), p. 17.
12. *New York Times* (1992, May 7).
13. Pool & Abelson (1961), pp. 167-183.
14. Jamieson (1992), p. 378.
15. Euchner & Maltese (1992), p. 289.
16. Jamieson (1992), p. 446.
17. Pomper (1988), p. 218.
18. Jamieson (1992), p. 468.
19. Jamieson (1992), p. 459.
20. McGinniss (1969), p. 35.

★2★

The Shifting Winds of Politics

Both Bill Clinton's and Ross Perot's campaign themes were spelled out in their respective books. Bill Clinton and Al Gore's book, titled *Putting People First: How We Can All Change America*, and Ross Perot's book, titled *United We Stand: How We Can Take Back Our Country*, center on empowering the voters to alter the course of events in this country. This same theme permeated each of their respective campaigns, which meant the candidates had to rely on consultants to get their names and messages out to the voters.[1]

It is becoming more expensive to create the name recognition necessary for candidates to bring in the kind of contributions and volunteer support that will help them defray the costs of running a modern-day presidential campaign. The numbers of dollars that have been spent on political advertising are staggering. Political advertising costs in 1984 totaled $153,824,000, as

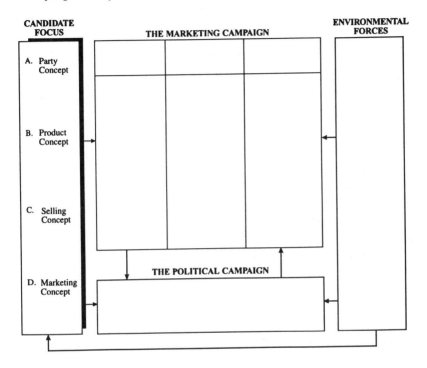

Figure 2.1. Candidate Focus in the Model of Political Marketing

compared to $227,900,200 in 1988, for an increase of 48.3%.[2] Computer technology has made the development of printed material easier and more cost effective, bringing about the increased use of direct mail, which can be targeted to groups of potential voters or contributors. But candidates realize that they must hire consultants, regardless of their fees, in order to stay competitive.

In this chapter, I develop the *candidate focus* component (see Figure 2.1) of the model of political marketing introduced at the beginning of the book. I will first discuss the forces behind the candidate's shift in focus from the party to the voter and consequent reliance on consultants and then contrast the party concept with the marketing concept, explaining how each concept affects the electoral process.

The Candidates Are Going Direct to the Voter

Marketing technology in the commercial marketplace has evolved over the last decade, with companies concentrating on building long-term relationships with their customers (referred to as relationship marketing). That is, companies are now taking their products and their message directly to the consumer without reliance on the standard channels of distribution. Dell, a computer company, for example, started out in the dormitory room of a college student whose genius surfaced in his use of a toll-free number to sell computers directly to consumers. The whole transaction was handled over the telephone with direct contact between the company and the consumer. In the process, Dell eliminated retailers, allowing Dell to cut their costs and offer a cheaper price to the end user.

The emphasis in relationship marketing is on using information technology to send targeted messages to specific segments of consumers. Companies like Dell have built up a database of information about their markets and essentially drive their business with the aid of this technology. Similarly, candidates now run their campaigns with the aid of computer technology. Because candidates have to rely on money to run their operations, fund-raising is also directed with aid from computers, with direct mail appeals sent to selected voter segments that are identified and stored in computer files.

The High Costs of Running for President

Presidential elections cost hundreds of millions of dollars to run these days. In part, this is due to the "high-tech" orientation that campaigns revolve around. Clinton's "war room" (what James Carville, his chief strategist, called their campaign headquarters in Little Rock, Arkansas) was reminiscent of a nerve center of any high-tech corporate office, with computers, televisions, and other technological gadgets used to monitor the information accumulating every minute of the day during the election. The cost and effort to keep up with what a candidate's opponents are saying in the media have become exorbitantly high. But it is critical to monitor competition to run an effective marketing campaign because any political campaign has at its heart two valves running through it, one keeping track of what the voters think and the other keeping track of what the competitors are saying.

An indication of the difficulty of winning a presidential election in the 1990s is the time involved, both in terms of the lead time before the campaign actually begins as well as the effort that needs to be exerted on a daily basis during the campaign. Clinton was considered by most accounts to be the best organized of all the Democratic nominees who started the primary season together. The same could be said for Jimmy Carter in 1976 or Ronald Reagan in 1980, the last two times a challenger from the opposing party won against a sitting incumbent. The race informally starts at least 2 years before the first primary, with some arguing that it starts the minute the previous election is over with posturing to influential groups both within and outside the political parties.

In addition, the media pose another hurdle to get over, as candidates try to work with influential power brokers in this industry to communicate their message and ensure that their image is crafted in a way that is consistent with the strategy of the campaign organization. This means that candidates must forge through grueling questioning about their personal and professional backgrounds.

An Older, Fragmented, and More Informed Electorate

Another force having an impact on the shift toward reliance on consultants is the sophistication and fragmentation of the electorate. The electorate is becoming more sophisticated and has more access to information than ever before, especially with the rising popularity of cable television, on which shows like C-Span had daily programming about events in the campaign. The pollsters now provide daily tracking polls to various media sources for voters to consume. The difficulty from the candidate's vantage point lies in crafting an image and message at different stages of the election that will appeal to the majority of voters. This creates a pressure for the candidate to "segment his market," or deliver different messages to different groups of voters and, at the same time, not step on any one voter group's toes.

In addition, American voters are getting older and have voted for and heard claims from several candidates over their voting lifetimes. They have witnessed how promises and claims are broken once a candidate takes office and, as a result, have become more skeptical. Not only are the voters cynical but the reputation of politicians is at an all time low, and the combination results in an electorate that does not respect politicians the way they used to. The more experienced and circumspect the voters, the more difficult it is to influence them, regardless of which power broker is trying to do the influencing. We see voters reading and paying more attention to the details of the campaign than ever before.

Today's voters are more diverse in their needs, as seen in the changing makeup of the population. People are more driven by individualistic life-styles today and, as a result, exhibit very unique consumption patterns. The definition of family as we know it is changing, as we witnessed from the attention paid to Murphy Brown, a single mother on the television show of that name. The issues surrounding *Murphy Brown* evoked strong reactions and was evidence of how sensitive the family issues area can be. There is a whole host of new voter segments that candidates must appeal to, including ethnic groups, socially concerned people, environmentalists, and others. The net result of voters' changing concerns is continued reliance on consultants to guide the candidate through the political campaign. Candidates have to have more marketing savvy than ever before, and they need to use strategic thinking, which consultants offer them.

Old Methods and Tactics Are Not Working

The old way of campaigning is not viable anymore; the party system as we know it can no longer be the sole basis on which to wage a campaign at the presidential level. This is not to say that grass-roots politics is dead in this country, but it does mean that candidates have more serious concerns than simply getting the nod of the party officials to run for president. Jimmy Carter, perhaps as no presidential contender before him, represents a good case example. A virtual outsider to Washington, Carter was able to campaign for this highest of offices without the graces of party insiders at the beginning of the primary season. With the aid of smart handlers, who understood the power of the marketing and strategic tools at their fingertips, Carter transcended party insider influence.

The campaign process is more complicated than it used to be, partly because issues are constantly changing. As we witnessed in the 1992 election, political bombshells can be dropped on candidates at any time, and, as a result, the candidates need experts who are adept at defusing these bombs and then reloading their own bombs almost instantaneously. Clinton used the media and, in particular, ABC's *Nightline* and other talk show formats, to retaliate against the seemingly nonstop barrage of accusations against his character and past record. Because of the advent of telemarketing, candidates cannot rely on the old way of doing business; just as corporations are adapting to new tools of the trade, so are campaign organizations.

The Decline of Party Loyalty

The independent candidacy of Ross Perot demonstrates well the loss of power of the two-party system in this country: On June 2, 1992, Perot, with no party backing, was on top in the polls, tied with Clinton for first place. Given the continued disconnection between voters and political parties, voters are looking at candidates differently. The parties themselves squabble internally and thereby weaken their own internal organization. The divisiveness caused by Pat Buchanan's speech at the Republican convention illustrates this point. The past three Democratic conventions also had signs of internal instability, as was evidenced by the infighting in 1980 between Edward Kennedy and Jimmy Carter and between Jesse Jackson and the party's nominee in both the 1984 and 1988 conventions. Part of the problem also stems from the political parties as they try to redefine themselves. In one CBS poll during the 1992 campaign, 28% of those polled called themselves Republicans, 31% called themselves Democrats, and 35% referred to themselves as Independents.[3]

Party loyalty has been on the decline in this country for some time now. This is not to say that voters do not cast a ballot on the basis of party loyalty, but it just isn't the same: Voters today take more time and effort to understand the issues of the campaign and are less likely to vote for a candidate on the sole basis of his party affiliation. Since Nixon's candidacy, the party is not as loyal to the candidate as it used to be. The comments of Washington insiders during the darker days of the Clinton campaign illustrate the waning loyalty: Several Congress members talked about the fact that Clinton was bringing too much baggage along with him and how he would only hurt the party. Today, the candidate cannot ride on the coattails of the party organization.

The Powerful Press

The press is one of the key power brokers in the political process. We have seen the emergence of investigative journalists (especially since Watergate and Vietnam) and the critical role they play in screening candidates. In effect, the press has become a watchdog, making it more difficult for candidates to hide their pasts. The voters want to know everything about a presidential candidate, from his personal life to his public utterances, and the press is in a position to satisfy the healthy voter appetite for this kind of information.

The press also has the benefit of technology to help it do its job. Nineteen ninety-two was the "year of the poll," with every major media outlet issuing instant information "snapshots" of the country on every imaginable issue. Part of this dramatic increase in the use of polls was due to the technological changes that have taken place in the industry. For example, the media have interactive capabilities: Television stations can commission a sample of voters to use their touch tone telephone to respond instantaneously to political commercials, debates, or speeches, and then the results can be reported on television within seconds.

Another issue deals with the immediacy of global news and the ability of the press to use political events taking place halfway around the world to shape the local news. During the last weeks of the 1992 election, there was talk of a coverup and manipulation of world events for political gain, namely, claims that George Bush allegedly used the Iraqi war for his own political purposes. The press becomes the channel through which global events are communicated to the voters. The opportunity now exists to have world leaders from other countries hooked up by satellite on news programs to talk about events that shape the political campaign.

Today's Press Is More Educated and Experienced

The education of the press has resulted in their use of new technologies to convey information in a more concise and packaged manner. The use of sophisticated market segmentation techniques, for example, allow journalists to report on the thinking and feeling of critical groups of voters. In other words, journalists carry out their own marketing research studies to determine voter responses. There is also the use of advanced methodologies in polling that enables the press to arrive at accurate predictions and explanations of the electorate's behavior and thinking.

The new rules on disclosure of campaign funding have made the candidate's organization an open book for journalists. This opportunity was unavailable 30 years ago when Kennedy ran for office. In addition, due to personal financial disclosures on candidates, the press can also peer into the personal backgrounds of the candidates in a different way than what was possible before.

Some argue that the influence that the press holds today is having a very strong effect on the political system. On the positive side is the view that there is more accountability in government now, but that view is countered with charges that the media trivialize the political process through the publication of rumors. The Gennifer Flowers fiasco is indicative of the quagmire the media can create.[4]

Along with a more experienced and educated press have come media that have the power of selectively influencing the public. A good example of this was the coverage of the Democratic convention: Different television stations left very different impressions with the viewers. On C-Span, the focus was on the speaker on the podium and the program included complete coverage of the day's events. The image reflected on C-Span was one of speakers with diverse backgrounds speaking their minds on the issues of the day. On the other hand, if the viewer was watching ABC, the coverage painted a picture of a different kind, with more attention paid to commentary by experts and politicians and less live coverage of the person speaking. In a word, ABC's coverage was much faster paced than was C-Span's, giving the viewer shots of the more exciting moments of the convention.[5]

A Brief Description and Evolution of the Marketing Concept

The evolution of the marketing concept is depicted in Figure 2.2, in which I outline the four stages that describe how presidential candidates have gone from campaign organizations run by party bosses to organizations run by marketing experts. The focus of the organization has also evolved from one that used to be centered on the political party to one centered on the voter.

If we look back to presidential elections up through the Eisenhower presidency, we see campaign organizations that followed the party concept. The organization had an internal focus (meaning that it operated on information

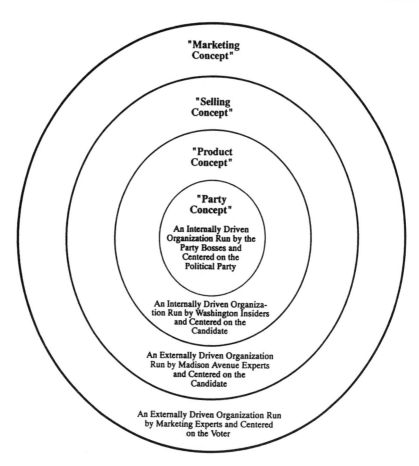

Figure 2.2. The Evolution of the Marketing Concept
NOTE: The focus of the political campaign or organization has evolved. Once centered on the political party, the political campaign became candidate-centered and then voter-centered.

generated from the people within the organization) and was run by party bosses whose only allegiance was to the political party. Grass-roots efforts to get the vote out were at the heart of the power of the political party, which is why someone like the late Mayor Richard Daley of Chicago wielded so much power within the party hierarchy. Daley successfully built up a "political machine" that could be tapped into at any time. The candidates at that time had no choice but to rely on the party bosses within the organization to become slated as a nominee.

In *The Making of the President*, Theodore White goes back to the Kennedy presidency to paint his picture of a changing electoral process, in which attention centered on the candidate instead of the political party. Efforts were made to surround Kennedy with the best and the brightest in Washington to make him as competitive as possible. In effect, White outlined what we in marketing have referred to as the *product concept*, which stresses the importance of manufacturing a quality product.[6] For example, efforts went into manufacturing the Model T Ford with only one idea in mind, namely, to build a quality automobile. Likewise, in politics the product concept would apply to campaign organizations that have only one idea in mind: to find the best possible candidate to represent the party. In contrast to the party concept in which allegiance is to the party, here it is directed to the candidate.

The next stage in the evolution of the marketing concept comes with a selling orientation, which was well outlined in *The Selling of the President*, by Joe McGinniss. In his book, McGinniss goes back to the Nixon presidency to describe how great efforts were taken to sell Nixon to the electorate by relying on media experts. Work went into making Nixon look as good as possible on television by using persuasive appeals in commercials to convince people to vote for him. We label this the *selling concept*, in which the focus of the campaign organization shifts from an internally to an externally driven operation. This is a significant shift in focus because it reflects the importance of relying on information generated from sources other than those within the campaign or party organization. Here the voter's reaction to the candidate's media appearances becomes critical. However, as with the product concept, the focus is still on the candidate.

The marketing concept goes a step further by first identifying consumer needs and then developing products and services to meet those needs. As pointed out before, the marketing concept centers on a very different philosophy than the party concept, the main difference being that the marketing concept centers on the consumer, in this case the voter, as the primary focus of the campaign. The delivery of promises once the candidate begins to govern is also pivotal to the philosophy behind the marketing concept.

There has been a recentering of focus onto the consumer in the business world because of the highly competitive marketplace in which companies operate. In order to avoid failure and ensure that consumers get what they want, companies must address their needs. This same orientation can be found in the political marketplace as well and is used to help the candidate avoid failure and win the election. With the aid of marketing experts, the candidate's organization takes on a whole new direction.

From a business perspective, the importance of following the marketing concept is well stated by Kotler:

> Some organizations have discovered the value of focusing their attention not on production, product, or sales, but on meeting their customers' changing needs and wants. They recognize that production, products, and sales are all means of producing satisfaction in target markets. Without satisfied customers, these organizations would soon find themselves "customer-less" and tailspin into oblivion.[7]

Similar logic can be applied to politics: We saw an incumbent president in 1992 who failed to recognize this important lesson.

As was pointed out before, the marketing concept differs from the product and selling concepts in several ways. First of all, the marketing concept begins with the voter not the candidate. Watching both Bush and Clinton test out several different campaign themes throughout the primaries in 1992 reinforced the notion that each was searching for the right "hot buttons" to use in their commercials. Second, as in business, developing a strategy around a product or selling concept is risky because there is no guarantee that what is produced will sell. Likewise, in politics, following a product or selling concept means the candidate looks no farther than his own ideology to develop the campaign platform, which may not be what the electorate wants to hear.

As in the business world, the marketing concept dictates what candidates do, and, as with businesses, candidates want to create and retain their customers. According to Peter Drucker, business has become organized around management, which is part of the backbone of today's political organizations. In modern political organizations, as in modern-day corporations, everybody has specialized knowledge in the mechanisms of marketing and computer technology.[8]

Are the Best Possible Candidates Running for Office?

When one carefully inspects who ran for the presidency in 1992, one wonders whether the better-known candidates in the Democratic party, such as Mario Cuomo, Richard Gephardt, and others, chose not to run because of Bush's standing in the polls at the start of the primary season. Based on this logic, one could argue that it was not the system that eliminated the better-known candidates from running but rather the competitive environment and the likelihood of winning or losing.

However, some political observers, participants, and others argue that the new rules of winning in presidential politics are driven by the new political technology and by the ability of a candidate to master it regardless of his credentials. If we look to the polls for evidence, we see there is a dissatisfaction with the election process currently used in this country. This was in part evidenced by the candidacy of Ross Perot, who was able to pull a coalition of dissatisfied voters together for 19% of the votes.

Of course, it is not completely fair to compare any candidate with Ross Perot: He was an election factor in large part because he was able to afford to spend $100 million on his campaign. When one compares this figure with the $106.5 million spent by or on behalf of Dukakis and the $93.7 million by Bush in 1988, it is no surprise that Perot made an imprint in the psyche of the American electorate.[9] An alternate explanation for the high percentage of votes garnered by Perot is that he tapped into the ultimate sense of volunteerism in America, a phenomenon seen in past campaigns in which the candidates relied on a volunteer network to get elected.[10]

Eventually, we will find out exactly what the Perot candidacy stood for. Some analysts and others argued that it will not be the first time people buy something they do not want or need. In fact, Perot has been referred to as a very slick salesman. Perhaps an even more important question is whether the Perot candidacy represented a frustrated electorate voicing their discontent with Washington. If that is the case, and Clinton does not perform well in office, we may see more of Perot in 1996.[11]

The Party Concept Versus the Marketing Concept

There are several differences between party-driven and voter-driven campaigns that have not yet been fully addressed. I have chosen several dimensions on which to compare the two alternative approaches, but by contrasting the two concepts it will become clear that the concept shift is here to stay.

Focus

Focus refers to the central aim and direction of the campaign organization. Similar to the blueprint of an architectural design of a house, the focus can be thought of as the blueprint of the campaign. Representing the overall mission of the campaign, focus sets the tone for the strategic and tactical decisions that the candidate makes throughout the political campaign.

Party Concept.   The first step of the development of a focus for the campaign begins with understanding the party hierarchy and functioning within the system in order to get standing, money, and grass-roots support. As with any organization, even though this one is loosely held, there are several levels of approval that a candidate goes through to become the nominee. The president becomes the flagship candidate who must carry other candidates on his coattails. Some media analysts observed that Bush lost his standing in the party at the same time his approval rating dropped in the polls, and several candidates running for Congress began to distance themselves from him. One indication of this distancing trend was the White House picture-taking ceremony, an opportunity for Congress members to come and have their picture taken with the president. Only a handful showed up, which in and of itself would not have been that bad, but the event was covered on the evening news.

The nominee who is eventually chosen to represent the party must be the best of all possible choices within the party or at least the most appealing and least threatening to party philosophy. At one point during the Democratic primaries, the leadership said that Clinton brought too much "dirty laundry" along with him, and, as a result, he was not seen as the most attractive candidate the party had to offer. Regardless of what the party officials thought, however, Clinton decided he was the best candidate, and, because of the new political technology, the party did not have the power to veto that decision.

Marketing Concept.   The first step in the marketing process is understanding the electorate and what it is looking for in a candidate. As with the party concept, this initial understanding helps the candidate to raise money, start a grass-roots support system, and achieve standing in the polls; standing in the polls is a virtual prerequisite for any candidate in today's elections who seeks to get to the top of the heap. There are layers within the process to go through here too, but in this case the candidate seeks assistance and consultation from the best possible pollster, media adviser, strategist, direct mail specialist, and other handlers who will implement the candidate's marketing strategy.

In some cases, the consultants will even go looking for the best candidate to fit the ideal image determined by the pollster or strategist from his or her marketing research. There are computer programs used to identify ideal prod-ucts for a given market based on research conducted with consumers. Likewise, this technology has been applied in political campaigns, where voters are surveyed and asked to identify the characteristics that represent their percep-tion of an ideal candidate. This is dangerous because it not only brings up a whole set of issues that have moral and ethical ramifications but also creates visions of candidates as empty vessels put in the water by handlers and then sailed into the White House without a reason for being there.

Objective

The *objective* is where marketing and politics merge into one another. The objective refers to the reason for the existence of the marketing system and the political system. The objectives of each system stem from their philo-sophical origins, however, which significantly differ.

Party Concept. According to this concept, the objective is to carry out the philosophy of the respective political party. Political science theory dictates how the system operates; in place for many years, procedures define the objectives of each of the two major political parties, each representing very different forms of democratic governance (i.e., liberal and conservative). According to the party concept, the campaign platform is subject to the dictates of the party hierarchy and to various powerful interest groups. The choice of candidate is determined by the officials who think the person can win and successfully carry out the dictates of the party.

Marketing Concept. The objectives here are first to win the election and then to deliver on the promises made in the campaign, both of which are accom-plished by satisfying voter needs. Perhaps the biggest criticism of this approach to politics is that a candidate can win an election and then never fulfill his promises once he gets into office. Therefore the objective of this concept is not properly fulfilled until the candidate carries out his promises once he is in office, assuming he wins.

Strategy

Strategy refers to the development of a planned approach to implementing the objective of the campaign organization. It centers on the tactical decisions that are made by the campaign workers on a day-to-day basis and incorporates the latest technology that the candidate's organization understands and can afford to use. The use of the media becomes a central tool in strategy, and, as we saw in the 1992 election, there have been some dramatic changes taking place.

Party Concept. Political parties for years have followed what has been referred to as "machine politics" to implement their objectives. This strategic orientation relies on the extensive use of a volunteer network or grass-roots operation to publicize the party's message, and the energies of the campaign are spent on making person-to-person contact with as many voters as possible. The successful implementation of this type of strategy is the result of the many "IOUs" that candidates acquire through a lifetime of loyal party affiliation. Bush is a classic example of a candidate whose political lifeblood was generated around this political orientation; he is a politician who held several posts in government throughout his life and did it with the help of many individuals. The basis for this strategic orientation stems from the party hierarchy. It begins with the National Committee at the top of the hierarchy and filters down to the state and local committees, which provide the grass-roots effort for the candidate.

Marketing Concept. In this case, strategy originates from the voter and begins by breaking down the electorate into distinct and separate segments of voters. Selected voter segments are then targeted with a specific message using an assortment of mass media techniques. Once the segments of voters are identified, the candidate creates an image for himself and uses that to position himself. The strategy is then executed through information channels based on the results of marketing research and polling.

Planning

Planning refers to the organizational procedures that are used to run the day-to-day activities of the campaign. There have been significant shifts in the planning approach, which is used to run campaign organizations and now seems closer to approaches in corporate organizations than in traditional campaign organizations.

Party Concept. Planning found in organizations run by the party concept is more operational than strategic. In other words, planning is more concerned about how to organize. It follows a more traditional approach to party management, in which the party structure determines how the plan is implemented. The candidate's organization is intimately linked to the national party hierarchy.

Marketing Concept. Here the orientation is more strategic in nature, with thinking that revolves around the future and competition. It begins with the voter as the basis for the development of a management information system and relies heavily on marketing research and polling to direct planning. This approach dictates that the candidate's organization operate independent of the national party organization but still in conjunction with it.

Corporate organizations have changed dramatically over the past decade, and these changes have permeated the very fabric of campaign organizations. Information and knowledge is used in creative ways to tie together the various operations of companies, and specialists have taken over the reins of power. The unique characteristic of organizations today is that they are flexible.

Structure

Structure refers to the way in which the organizational chart is organized and the chain of command within the campaign organization. Issues such as people selection, assigning tasks to individuals, and implementing, monitoring, and controlling the activities of the organization come into play here.

Party Concept. The structure is highly centralized under the party concept, with the control and management of the whole organization centered around a single person or two. The national party chair has a tremendous amount of influence and in effect runs the show, keeping internal divisions to a minimum and making sure that the best nominee is chosen to represent the party. The candidate's own campaign organization is well integrated into the party organization.

Marketing Concept. Here the focus is much more decentralized, with areas of responsibility given to different people at different stages during the campaign, again as a function of voter response. Various duties are delegated to certain people, with top people directing or supervising. As a rule, the candidate has his own team of professionals running the organization. Under this concept, the party organization is not well integrated into the candidate's organization, almost to the point of exclusion in some cases. Political organizational structure follows structural innovations now found in business, in which the internal functions between people are blurred and the organization strives to operate as a team.

Advertising and Promotion

Advertising and promotion have changed dramatically in politics. The campaign button and automobile bumper sticker have been replaced by a variety of innovative media, including videotapes of the candidate that highlight his background and experiences, infomercials that devote 30 minutes of paid advertising time to deliver detailed messages to voters, and satellite hookups to several local television stations that simultaneously broadcast interviews. There has also been a shift in funds to local cable stations, through which candidates can more effectively and efficiently target and send their message to potential voters.

Party Concept. The orientation here revolves around the candidate and the party. This orientation permeates every aspect of the promotional strategy, especially in terms of the campaign platform put forth to the electorate. The candidate becomes more preoccupied with the party's philosophy than with his own, and thus he is defined in terms of party ideology.

Marketing Concept. This approach revolves around the voter, with an emphasis on using media outlets and message appeals that are based on results reported from the marketing research and polling. The candidate defines himself based on his own terms and philosophy, and primaries serve as test markets to determine message appeals. Test markets are similarly used by companies who pass out free samples of new products to determine if demand is great enough for full-scale production. An emphasis is placed on consistency of message, with all promotional vehicles strategically linked together.

Conclusion

This chapter has examined the shift that has taken place in politics from a party orientation toward a marketing orientation. Along with this shift, there have been several developments in the way political campaigns are run, the most important of which is the integration of a marketing campaign into a political campaign, which in turn shifts focus from the party to the voter. Political campaign organizations are run by consultants today, with flexible organizational styles that enable the candidate to respond almost instantaneously to events that take place.

Candidates have been forced to rely on marketing specialists due to several forces in the political environment, including a more powerful press, political parties in decline, and an electorate that is more fragmented and sophisticated. The net result of these forces is found in the growing similarities between political and business organizations. Several indicators support the fact that the shift is here to stay. In the next chapter, I inspect how the shift just outlined has affected those who really control the electoral process in this country.

Notes

1. Clinton & Gore (1992), p. 1; Perot (1992), p. 3.
2. Alexander (1992), p. 85.
3. *The New York Times* (1992, June 2).
4. Sabato (1991), p. 208.
5. *The New York Times* (1992, July 16).
6. White (1982), p. 165.
7. Kotler (1982), p. 22.
8. Drucker (1986), p. 119.
9. *The New York Times* (1992, April 24).
10. *Time* (1992, May 25), p. 26.
11. *Time* (1992, November 2), p. 47.

★3★

The Powers That Be

Several forces in the political environment have an impact on those who now control the political campaign process (see Figure 3.1). The shift in power in politics has resulted from two basic forces, namely, from technology and structural shifts in the political process. The three influential areas of innovation in technology include the computer, television, and direct mail. Each of these areas directly affects the way presidential candidates run their campaigns, forcing candidates to utilize the expertise of marketing specialists who can guide them through the intricate maze that accompanies the innovations.

The structural shifts influence primary and convention rules, financial regulations, and debates. Complex primary and convention rules have altered the way candidates run for the presidency. Ross Perot's attempt to get on the ballot in all 50 states created an administrative nightmare for his organiza-

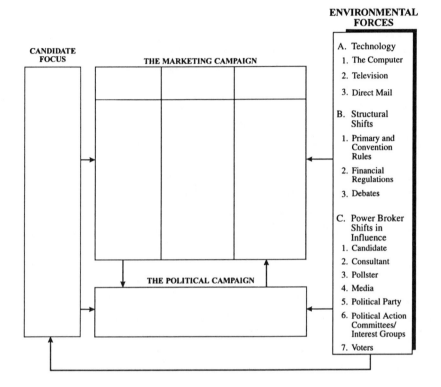

Figure 3.1. Environmental Forces in the Model of Political Marketing

tion, reflecting the difficulty for an independent candidate to run for president. Likewise, limitations on individual contributors have forced candidates to rely on not only fund-raising experts but direct mail experts as well.

Advances in direct mail technology have given candidates the ability to carefully target selected voter blocs with the appropriate messages, and their campaigns are no longer solely financed by the coffers of national party headquarters but are dependent on individual contributors. These shifts have further pressured candidates to rely on the expertise of direct mail wizards to navigate through each stage of the political campaign. The technological and structural changes that are covered in this chapter have resulted in dramatic shifts in influence among the power brokers. To fully understand the analysis that will be presented in Part II, we now need to turn to the forces that have been responsible for the transformation of the electoral process.

Technology

As technology in campaigning changes, so does the reliance on marketing experts, who know the intricacies of different technologies. Computer hardware and software advances enabled the candidates to go directly to the voter in 1992. Some of the applications of technological advances, discussed previously, include database marketing, direct marketing, fund-raising, polling, and teleconferencing.

The Computer

The computer, more than any other innovation, provided the power brokers with a forceful tool that was used to change the course of political campaigns. For example, the use of computers allowed the television media, for the first time during the course of the 1992 election, to get immediate responses to candidate speeches and campaign commercials. The Gallup organization in concert with the ABC news program *Nightline* selected a random sample of voters to participate in a live interview. By simply pushing buttons on their telephones, respondents were able to respond to the comments made by the candidates during one of the debates. *Nightline* then reported the results of the interview survey instantaneously on television. The television program used a colored chart for millions of viewers to see a graphic representation of the responses of this select group of voters.

During the course of this campaign, consultants used the computer in much the same way as they had for years. Perhaps its primary use is as a database for names, phone numbers, and addresses of tens of thousands of voters, grouped according to their views and demographic characteristics. This file becomes the basis for fund-raising and direct mail campaigns to solicit money for the campaign "war chest." The computer is also used to analyze the results of marketing research studies that are carried out by campaign organizers.

Pollsters apply computer technology to conduct an abundance of polls throughout the course of a campaign. The pollsters work for the candidates, using polling technology to generate statistical snapshots of the twists and turns of the campaign. They also work for the media, using their skills as a way of attracting voter interest in the horse race mentality of the campaign. Political action committees and lobbyists also count on computers to gauge the strength of their single-issue causes. Finally, voters who form coalitions take advantage of this technology to fine-tune their grass-roots efforts.

Furthermore, new computer services allow campaign organizations to examine Federal Election Commission reports on any campaign, political action committee, or political party. Database systems are being developed that allow the user to perform research that once had to be performed by hand. In the 1992 election, candidates continued to use a computer service offered to interested parties called the Presidential Campaign Hotline. According to Frank Luntz,

> The Presidential Campaign Hotline provides presidential candidates and the news media with the latest political information, analysis, polls, and gossip for a certain fee per month, and also allows the subscriber to down load a daily fifteen to thirty page report that features exclusive material issued by the presidential campaigns, and an insiders summary of important political events.[1]

This technology comes at a time when computerization of voter registration lists for almost every state, city, and town is complete, which enables campaign organizations to target specific voter groups in any district they select. As a result of this development in computer technology, political survey research has become more accurate and precise at a lower cost to the candidate. Both polling methodology and analytical techniques have undergone significant refinements in the past decade.[2]

Luntz has written extensively on several of the technological advances used in the 1988 election, including the so-called Perception Analyzer. This device is used by putting respondents into groups of 50 to 100 people, each one of whom is provided with a handheld computer linked to a device that has a numbered dial. Respondents are then asked to turn the dial based on whether they get a negative impression or a favorable impression, which in turn gives the users immediate feedback.[3] This new polling technique was also used in the 1992 campaign.

Television

Technological advances in television can be found in several areas but especially in the cable industry. Television became the platform from which grass-roots fund-raising efforts were conducted, beginning with Jerry Brown's television campaign to develop his volunteer network and then Perot's similar effort to develop his mailing list of volunteers. Brown and Perot used a tactic modeled after late-night television advertisements, in which an announcer gives out an "800" number to call to order the latest in vegetable-cutting technology or other products sold direct to the consumer.

Superstations for cable television that use satellites for national distribution of their programming have turned into one of the most effective broadcast outlets for candidates. Broadcasting has replaced newspapers as the central mass communication outlet, but because of the incongruence between political boundaries and media markets defined for television, targeting becomes more difficult.[4] With newspapers, the demographic boundaries are much better defined because newspapers have a smaller, more localized audience. Television and radio, on the other hand, sometimes transmit to even national audiences, making it difficult to target specific messages.

Media and marketing specialists looking to the future have suggested that the new media will allow the currently disenfranchised citizen greater access to political information. But another observation on modern communications is that it will further aggravate the problem of factions in American politics. Most, however, agree that the mass media have gradually replaced party organizations as the principal conduits between the voters and the candidate.[5]

In their book *The Electronic Commonwealth*, Abramson, Arterton, and Orren note that with more interactive media candidates will be able to better respond to the concerns of individual citizens. Much of the activity discussed about this new technology involves efforts by politicians to bypass the gatekeeping function that journalists exercise over political discourse. This is a step toward a more direct, less mediated form of politics. National interest groups are now able to reach their membership directly, bypassing the local and state affiliates that formerly filtered their messages. Citizens no longer need to wait until the dinner hour for network anchors to tell them what happened in the campaign; candidates can be seen on a regular basis on cable television.[6]

Direct Mail

Direct mail is used in four key ways: to promote issues, programs, and candidates; to mobilize public pressure on political leaders; to raise money; and to recruit new members for citizen action groups. The emergence of direct mail for recruiting and mobilizing the public into national action groups and for generating political fund-raising has created substantial alarm among many people. However, more voters are participating in politics through direct mail, and therefore one could argue it is a positive force on the political process.[7]

As previously discussed, candidates rely on databases to target their appeals to specific segments of voters and to build a more intimate rapport with the voters by sending direct mail information to the voters in their own names. Mail that is addressed to a person by name adds a personal touch that can induce the receiver to open the envelope before it is thrown out. Briefly alluding to the use of this technology before, I referred to it as "relationship marketing." Relationship marketing is a strategic orientation that views the consumer with a long-term perspective. This orientation is implemented in the commercial marketplace by customizing products, personalizing promotional appeals, creating flexible pricing policies, and going direct to the consumer. All of these activities are carried out to better satisfy consumers' needs. Likewise, we see the same orientation filtering into the political marketplace.

Relationship marketing is built in three stages. The first stage incorporates the identification and constant updating of a database of information about the consumer or voter. The amount or type of information that can be stored is limited only by the software and hardware being used and the imagination and creativity of the person developing the files. Second, the information is used to target specific appeals and messages to the voter in a very personal way; that is, direct mail literature that comes to the voter's door soliciting funds would be addressed to the voter by name. Once the database is developed, it becomes imperative that it be updated to reflect a baseline of information about the most valuable voters, such as those who contribute over a certain dollar amount.[8]

Direct mail is a powerful political tool because it provides candidates with technical advantages that no other promotional tool can match, such as test marketing, personalizing a message, targeting a message, and instantaneous feedback. As the movement toward relationship marketing grows in politics, so will the dependence on this technology.

Structural Shifts

We have seen some dramatic changes taking place in the way in which the electoral process is structured. The shifts I will discuss have affected three areas: primary and convention rules, financial regulations, and debates. The primary and convention rules have affected the nominating procedure, which must be followed by candidates in their respective parties. Both major parties have very different rules that govern how they operate. Another change is reflected in the financial regulations instituted in recent years that limit contributions to candidates and parties, putting more pressure on candidates to develop mass media fund-raising appeals. Finally, significant changes surfaced in the debate process in 1992; among the most significant was the inclusion of voters to direct questions to the candidates.

Primary and Convention Rules

There have been several structural changes in the political system that have spurred on the merging between politics and marketing. The voters in every primary are different because states in different parts of the country have different agendas and demographic makeups. In addition, the primary voter varies from the general election voter and therefore forces the candidate to adapt his strategy as he moves through the stages of the political campaign. Similarly, as the candidate moves from one primary to another, appeals may change as candidates' ratings in the polls ebb and flow. Although it takes one kind of message and image to win the nomination, a more centrist appeal is needed to win the general election.

Since the 1968 convention, the Democrats have amended their nominating process every four years. In some years, the Democrats have virtually overhauled their process, while in other years the changes have been relatively minor. At the core of these changes has been the desire on the part of the party to devise a system that encourages grass-roots participation. Because the two parties operate under different sets of rules, each has very different assessments of the degree of change made in the opposing party.[9]

Winning a nomination now requires participation by the candidate in every primary and caucus, while the number of presidential primaries has increased to close to 40. The winner-take-all systems of allocating delegates, which the Republicans allow, have enabled the Republicans to wrap up their nominating contests quickly in the last several presidential elections.[10]

As a result of having lost in six of the last seven presidential elections, the Democrats decided to alter their approach to the convention in 1992. This included avoiding the perception that linked Bill Clinton and Al Gore to the Democrats of the last seven presidential campaigns. To accomplish this, Clinton and Gore removed themselves from the traditional causes that come from labor unions and other traditionally liberal interest groups. In 1992 the Democrats made some significant shifts in the party platform, including their endorsement of rights for gays and lesbians, higher taxes on the rich, and other programs affecting abortion and child care. These are not the programs one would have seen at recent conventions but reflect some structural shifts in the electorate that find fewer factory workers and more teachers and government workers belonging to labor unions.

In order for candidates to appear on a primary ballot they must follow a very complicated process. To appear on the New York State ballot, for example, where the laws are the most complex in the country, a Democratic candidate must collect 10,000 signatures or more from registered Democratic voters. And a minimum of 100 of the signatures must be from each of the congressional districts, of which there are 34.[11]

In fact, there was not a Republican primary in New York in 1992 because of Patrick Buchanan's inability to meet the requirements of the state's election rules. Buchanan's situation reflects the power of the incumbency as well as the clout of the state party to protect a sitting Republican president.[12]

Little did Perot know what he was in for when he began his presidential bid, which began with a struggle to come to grips with the varying and complex primary laws from state to state. For example, not only do states differ in the number of signatures required on petitions but the two-party system that we have was built to keep out third-party candidates. Hence we recall the famous words of Perot, "Get me on the ballot of all 50 states and I'll run for president." Some states even require certain kinds of paper to be used and that the petitions be stapled a certain way.[13]

One of the strongest indications of how well our democracy is working is the level of participation of the electorate. One of the paradoxes of U.S. presidential elections is that as more and more citizens acquire the right to vote, a smaller percentage of them exercise that right. This is the result of more restrictive laws dealing with registration and voting, which often prevent citizens from going to the polls.

Financial Regulations

There are a whole host of issues that have shaped the course of events in political campaigns with regard to financial regulations. First of all, elections are becoming more costly. With the use of sophisticated marketing techniques comes the high cost of consultants to carry out marketing functions. The campaign's duration has lengthened, with candidates starting their campaign sometimes 2 to 3 years ahead of the primaries.

In presidential campaigns, the large number of primary election contests and the increased length of the nomination campaign period have also added to rising costs of campaigns. Campaign finance reforms enacted in 1974 further prolonged the prenomination campaign period and, as a result, increased the costs to campaign organizations. Therefore, because candidates can no longer rely on large contributors to cover campaign costs, they generally begin their fund-raising at early stages to generate enough money from many small contributors.

The 1976 campaign was the first election regulated by finance reform legislation enacted in 1971 and 1974. The Federal Election Campaign Act (FECA) of 1971 limited campaign expenditures and required disclosure of campaign expenditures.[14] In the 1980 election, although Carter's and Reagan's spending was capped by federal law, additional expenditures were allowed by independent committees based on a 1976 Supreme Court ruling: "Approximately 12 million dollars was spent by independent groups for Reagan; less than $50,000 was spent for Carter. In 1980 Reagan spent $18,476,000 of his federal allocation on advertising, but garnered benefits from over $30,000,000." [15]

The political campaign process is governed by several different financial regulations that were enacted since the 1988 presidential campaign. These include

the itemization of expenses exceeding $200 or more and the listing of contributors giving at least $200;

limitations of donations made by an individual to $1,000 for each presidential candidate, $5,000 for any one political action committee, and $20,000 for the national committee of a political party, not to exceed a total of $25,000.

In addition, presidential candidates able to raise $100,000 in individual contributions, with at least $5,000 raised in 20 different states, may receive matching funds equal to the total contributions in amounts of $250 or less.[16]

These regulations affect candidates because of the importance of winning the early primaries. As a result of their desires to win in initial primaries and caucuses, candidates are predisposed to heavy spending in the early stages of a campaign. However, once the general election comes around, public financing is given to nominees of the major parties, namely, the candidates who won 25% or more of the popular vote in the last presidential election. In order to be eligible for federal money, the nominees must agree not to use or accept other campaign contributions in their campaign. Candidates of minor parties, that is, those who won between 5% and 25% of the vote in the previous election, receive partial public financing.[17]

Since the 1970s, presidential candidates have begun to raise money for their campaigns before state elections begin, and canvassing of funds continues during the general campaign period. Candidates who do not do well in the first primaries tend to drop out of the race early as a result of the finance laws. Under the campaign finance law, federal matching funds are cut off within 30 days if a candidate garners less than 10% of the votes in two consecutive primaries. Therefore candidates must decide not only how to raise funds but also how to spend them.

Even if presidential candidates decide not to take any federal matching money from the government, they are still bound by laws. Even though Perot did not accept any federal money for his campaign, he was still bound by a law that prevented a presidential candidate from receiving more than $5,000 from any political action committee and more than $1,000 from any individual voter in the general election.[18]

The Debates

Debates historically have been the avenue through which voters find real insight into the candidates' leadership abilities. One misstep in a debate, and the chances for election could be all over. For example, in the 1976 debates between Jimmy Carter and Gerald Ford, Ford claimed that Eastern European nations did not consider themselves to be under the domination of the Soviet Union. Luster lies in the high stakes of a debate, where a single misstatement of fact could ruin a candidate's chances for winning the election.

In 1992, as in the past, there was debate over the debates. However, something very different happened in the 1992 debates: The second debate included uncommitted voters asking the candidates questions. Moderated by Carol Simpson, a television journalist, this was a first in presidential debates. As usual, the moderator in the debate had power over creating images that are critical at this stage in a campaign. Carol Simpson, for example, made a lasting impression by referring to George Bush as "the education president" at one point in the debate or to Perot as someone who has an answer for everything. Even though these comments might not be intended to be sarcastic, they do create images in voter minds that are difficult to erase.

That second debate format was negotiated by Clinton's organization, which wanted its candidate to have the opportunity to meet his opponents in an electronic town meeting format, one he was very familiar with. It was the element of surprise in this debate format that Clinton's organizers felt would showcase their candidate, who was considered by many to be much quicker on his feet than Bush. In fact, the strategy worked; Clinton not only shined but Bush did not perform well because he seemed ill at ease and slightly defensive when responding to some of the questions posed by the voters.

The influence of the debates on both the political and marketing campaigns is enormous. Clinton wanted to use the debates to help voters to envision him sitting in the oval office of the White House. That meant he had to keep his answers short and to the point and not fight with his opponents, a goal he ultimately accomplished.

Bush's people spelled out their conditions for the debate format and refused to debate at all if Clinton did not go along with their stipulations. Clinton wanted to follow the format suggested by the independent commission on debates, which called for three debates and only one moderator asking the questions at each debate, but Bush did not agree out of fear that the moderator for one of the debates would be impartial. Finally, their compromise resulted in this innovative format of voters asking the questions in one of the debates, a structural change that will more than likely become a fixture in the debate formats of future presidential elections.

The Power Brokers

The debates lead us to a discussion of who now controls the presidency and how that control has shifted over the last several campaigns. Who are the power brokers in politics today? As was pointed out in chapter 1, there are seven players who affect the political process in elections today: the candidates, consultants, pollsters, media, political action committees and interest groups, political parties, and voters. Each one of these groups represents a different base of power that has altered the political reality in the United States. I refer to these participants as power brokers because each affects and

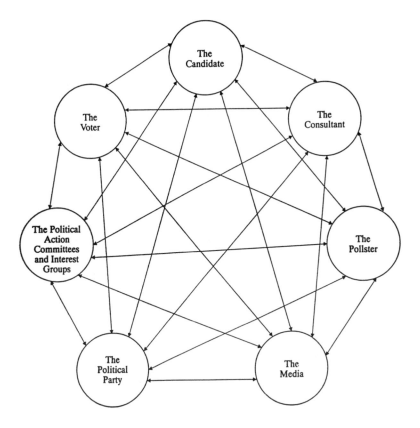

Figure 3.2. The Power Brokers in Politics in the 1990s
NOTE: Each of the seven power brokers affects the electoral process by influencing the others.

is affected by the other, and, more important, each one has a direct impact on marketing and political campaigns (see Figure 3.2). Power is what is being sought out through politics, and these participants influence and decide who has it and how it is used. The 1992 election showed a continuing and significant shift in power within the political process.

The Candidate

Most candidates enter into politics with a philosophy and ideological slant that influence their positions on the issues. This means that the candidate needs to blend and balance the research findings and his ideology. As pointed out before, the candidates rely more and more on polling and focus groups to direct their campaign platform development.

The 1992 presidential election presented three very different candidates, each with his own brand of politics. Clinton, the governor, appealed to Americans with a platform based on change and building up the economy again. Bush was the incumbent who promised to offer the American public stability and global security and referred to the Iraqi war as evidence of his ability to carry out his claim. However, at the same time, Bush tried to create fear in the minds of the voters that Clinton did not have the moral fiber to lead the country and, if put into a crisis situation, would not be able to handle himself.

Finally, there was an outsider who penetrated the two-party system and got equal footing with the other two candidates in the presidential debates. As a political outsider, Perot offered Americans a candidate who was non-traditional. Perot presented himself as a man of action who had the experience and ability to solve the country's problems, and he challenged Americans to face up to the realities facing their country.

As marketing campaigns continue to influence the political campaign, candidates will acquire more influence to become the captains of their own vessels. In today's political waters, it is the candidate who must make the final decisions on the course that is charted for his campaign. In 1992 Clinton became the candidate to prove his control in running his own campaign.

The Consultant

The continual rise in influence of consultants, or handlers, in presidential campaigns has expanded the importance of the role they play in modern-day politics. These new professionals have carved out a niche for themselves that makes them virtually indispensable to the candidate. The consultants essentially work with the candidate to fine-tune his message and image and communicate his vision of the country's future to the people.

James Carville, Clinton's top strategy adviser, was able to simplify Clinton's message and help him impart it effectively to the American people. Many political analysts argue that the consultant has taken over the ranks of the party bosses and now shapes the electoral process. Even before announcing that he is running for the presidency, a candidate finds out who he is able to recruit onto his consulting team. The consultants drive the campaign organization and cover several areas of expertise one would likely find in a corporate organization.

Modern campaign technology has complicated the lives of the candidates, who now see the role of consultants as a legitimate professional activity. Any candidate running for president must use consultants for essential services such as survey research, fund-raising, and advertising. Consultants are also used by political action committees and the national party organization. Consultants consider several factors in their decision to work for a client, including the candidate's ideology, electability, and personal wealth. Furthermore, presidential campaigns offer instant credibility and fame for firms fortunate enough to be on the winning side.[19]

In a survey by Frank Luntz sent out to political consultants of the 1970s and 1980s, the two greatest changes in campaigning cited in the past decade were television and the change in election laws.

> The Federal Election Campaign Act of 1971, the 1974 Campaign Law (also known as the FECA amendments), and the amendments of 1976 and 1979, all of these legislative acts placed strict limits on individual campaign contributions, required public disclosure of major contributors and expenditures, regulated the financial involvement of the political parties in the campaigns of their candidates, legalized the formation of political organizations representing organized labor and large corporations, and created a federal organization, the Federal Election Commission (FEC), with the legal power to enforce the new rules.

The irony is that the reform legislation of the 1970s, which was designed to open up the political process and reduce the impact of rich contributors and special interest groups, actually put pressure on candidates to rely on the services of political consultants.[20]

The Pollster

Never before have we seen such a proliferation of polls conducted throughout the course of a presidential campaign than in 1992. In fact, the polls became as much the focus of the election as the candidates or their messages were. In the past, it was not uncommon for campaign organizations to incorporate polls and standard marketing research data into campaign development and candidate image building. In fact, use of polling and marketing research are the most significant ways in which candidates are adapting marketing to their campaigns. However, with the continual rise in popularity of polling techniques, the implications of their use must be examined.

The argument against the proliferation of polls makes the point that they increase the horse race mentality of the campaign, which takes the focus off the issues and even dissuades some people from voting if they think their candidate does not have a chance. Or, in the case of Perot, polls spotlighted the candidate when he shot up to top rankings in the summer. In fact, some voters argued that a vote for Perot was a wasted vote because, according to the polls, he had no chance of winning. The argument in favor of the proliferation of polls contends that they give more information and feedback to voters to make more informed choices and thus help strengthen democracy. This is an issue that should be looked at very seriously and will continue to be debated.

Another important question regarding polling is not whether polling in general can be trusted but whether a specific poll can be trusted. This places a special burden on all those who report on polls to acquire the knowledge needed to evaluate the poll's methodology and the limits to which its findings can be generalized to the population as a whole.[21]

Again, the most serious issues here revolve around the impact of polling on democracy. There will be arguments in favor of the role of pollsters because they allow all voters to get a snapshot view of the campaign as it progresses. However, at the same time, the issues of accuracy and trust that were raised earlier will continue to come into play in future elections. Most likely, pollsters will continue to play a role as key power brokers controlling the political process.

The Media

The media played a very significant role in the 1992 election and set the stage for several innovations that will be in place for presidential elections to come. One significant change that took place involved the role of investigative journalists such as Sam Donaldson and Ted Koppel. In past elections, these journalists were the standard bearers of news who helped the public to pick and choose its political leaders. But since the political party's continuing decline in this country, the investigative arm of the media has played a new role in politics. In a sense, the media have served as the "check and balance" on the character and background of the candidates running for office, especially the presidential office. One only needs to think back to the Roger Mudd interview with Ted Kennedy to understand the power and influence of the media. When Kennedy was asked a simple question by Roger Mudd, namely, why he wanted to be president, Kennedy could not answer. That interview in the summer of 1980 immediately killed Kennedy's candidacy.

Since that time, the media continue to play an increasingly important role in screening would-be candidates for president. More often than not, the reporters grill the candidates about anything from sexual activities (e.g., the *60 Minutes* interview with Clinton and his wife Hillary) to patriotism (e.g., the *Nightline* interview with Clinton in which he was questioned about a letter he had written 20 years ago stating his opposition to the Vietnam War). However, during the course of the 1992 election, the investigative reporter's role was supplemented by talk show hosts, who provided live formats, including both call-in and audience participation, for the candidates to speak directly to the voters' concerns. Clinton is credited as being the first candidate, during the 1992 primaries (in New Hampshire), to use an audience participation format. From this followed a series of talk show formats that were used by all of the candidates.

Several issues regarding the role of the media in elections need to be brought to light here. First there is the issue of fairness and whether the media did a fair job of reporting the 1992 campaign to the American public. Second, the issue arises as to whether or not the media should have the responsibility they currently do. A third issue deals with the newly found prominence of Larry King and other talk show hosts. And a fourth issue deals with the way in which the Clinton campaign successfully used the media to aggressively attack crises by going onto television to rebuke the claims made against him.

More voters get their news from television than from any other media source. In campaigns today, the competition is as fierce between the media as it is between the candidates. But each has assets that meet the needs of the other: Candidates are in need of exposure that only the media can provide, and the media need inside information about the candidates that only sources in the campaigns have. As a result, each strives to control the conditions under which the candidates are presented to the electorate. Both the media and the campaign organizations are vulnerable to the control of the other.[22]

The increase in the number of interest groups in recent years, combined with the decline in political party influence and affiliation, has increased the importance of the news media. Because of their new status and influence in policy agenda setting through the formation of public opinion, the news media need to look at their role more carefully. They represent a variety of interests to society. The media do more than just pass on the agendas of candidates; they amplify and legitimize the candidates' agendas.[23]

So how fair were the media to Clinton? Some say they did a great job in hounding Clinton throughout his campaign about every aspect of his past. However, Clinton's aggressive use of the same media allowed him to confront head on those who tried to push him out of the race. One would have to argue that the media will play an increasingly important role in modern-day politics and, as power brokers in the system, must be held accountable to a high code of ethics.

The Political Party

The political parties in this country still command the respect of candidates running for president. Although the role of the political parties has diminished over the last several presidential elections, if one looks at the role they play in financing presidential candidates' campaigns in the general election, one can see that they are still a serious power broker.

At the presidential level, the party chair works with the campaign organization in a facilitating role. The party essentially acts as a conduit between the voter and the candidate, soliciting money, contributions, and time from people to be redistributed to candidates in much the same way that a corporation funnels money and effort to the brand managers of its products.

Parties exercise political power through the support they provide for candidates running for public office and by seeking out the views of their most powerful members. One of the distinctive functions of political parties was formerly the selection of candidates and the campaigning activities provided for them. However, due to changes in the rules of delegate selection, this function has transferred to the consultants. Because candidates are now self-selected and campaign for themselves through the media, there has been a decline in the power of parties.

One explanation for the decline in party influence in presidential elections is that parties are not perceived to be in a position to solve the most important domestic and foreign policy issues that confront the nation. In the voters' minds, the parties are losing their association with candidates and the issues that the candidates advocate.

Political parties, along with national elections, have been the hallmarks of modern democracy, and thus some have equated the political party with a place for the voters to hang their hats. However, the political party has become little more than one of many groups that participate in elections. Consequently, candidates have asserted their independence from party leaders.[24]

Polls and ticket splitting support the fact that party identification has faltered in this country. Polls indicate that the percentage of voters who identify with either major party has dropped, whereas voters who identify with neither of the major parties has increased. Correspondingly, the number of people who vote a split ticket has significantly increased. The role of party leaders has also changed from one of active participation to one in which a leader must first be invited by the candidate to participate. For example, at the Democratic convention and afterward Clinton made a point of not appearing with well-recognized Democrat leaders to distance himself from the negative attitudes voters have toward Washington insiders.[25]

However, the increasing number of political action committees has given the parties a new role. In effect, the parties have become political action committees on a grand scale, and in this capacity they offer candidates money and expertise. Both of the major parties send out political action committee bulletins every month in an attempt to raise money for their candidates. They instruct the political action committees about which races are serious and where they should direct their efforts. Also, the two national parties now have political action committee experts on their payrolls. In this manner, the national parties can still provide extra political clout in years when the public is looking for a change.[26]

The probability of collapse of the party system in this country is debatable, but its role is visibly changing. The party still plays a crucial function for the presidential nominee of the party in the form of finances and grass-roots distribution efforts, such as volunteer networks. However, even for the nominee, the extent to which the party mechanism is used is diminishing. Unlike in campaigns of the past, party bosses do not choose the nominees anymore. We now have a primary system that presents the structural opportunity for the candidate to rely on marketing experts to win the nomination even before it gets to the convention. In other words, there is evidence that this country is moving from an internally driven, party-oriented system to an externally driven, consumer-oriented system.

The party's diminishing power is more apparent when one looks at the candidacy of Perot. A candidate with no party affiliation, Perot made his independent candidacy a selling point in his campaign, telling the voters that something was wrong with this country, namely, its political process, and that voters needed to take their country back from the Washington insiders.

Political Action Committees and Interest Groups

These power brokers function in a very important capacity to influence the other power brokers in the process. The political action committees harness the power of individual voters to create a stronger voice and direct collected money to their favorite candidates. The lobbyists perform the same function for corporations and other organizations whose agendas often center on the health and strength of the organization that is being represented.

From a marketing perspective, these power brokers shape not only the development of campaign appeals made by the candidate but also the decision-making by segments of voters. Political action committees that represent pro-life and pro-choice issues, for example, solicit money from supporters and then funnel that money into the campaign "war chest" of the candidates who support their causes. These committees engage in marketing by conducting their own simple and informal surveys of the major candidates and the issues and then redistributing the results to their constituencies. This took place, for example, with a group representing the pro-life lobby that asked each of the three candidates to respond to a series of questions; the interest group then distributed the results in the form of a brochure to churches throughout the country.

Interest groups are organizations that advocate for or against one or more issues or policies of government and institute a structure to their demands to have an impact on the views of the candidates. Interest groups with a large membership base place the most emphasis on public relations as a technique for influencing action. Members may be called on to contribute to the group's strength by giving money, writing letters to party officials, demonstrating, or voting for the group's designated candidates. Most important, interest groups influence the political process through their financial contributions to election campaigns.[27] One concern is not whether to eliminate the influence of interest groups but how to make their power more equitable.

As a result of the increasing number of interest groups in Washington, there has been a greater need for the use of public relations consultants, fund-raising experts, and public opinion pollsters. More than three quarters of Washington interest groups use the services of public relations consultants. Organizations representing various interests in Washington have cropped up over the last two decades, mirroring the changes that have taken place in the political parties. As opportunities for public participation in politics at the national level have increased, group loyalties have become more important as a basis for political behavior. Hence one can see how political action committees and interest groups has influenced the role of marketing in the political process and why they have the control they do over candidates.[28]

The Voters

The last of the power brokers are the voters, who have the ultimate power in the political process if that power is harnessed in a structured and organized way. Several voter groups formed coalitions around the country to voice their concern about the candidates' campaign platforms. For example, gays and lesbians formed a partnership with Clinton and brought him a voting bloc on election day that contributed to his winning the election. The electorate is differentiated from the political action committees because many voters do not support political action committees and interest groups representing their views but will still vote for a particular candidate.

Ultimately, the voters are the key power brokers in the political process in much the same way that consumers are power brokers in the commercial marketplace. The voters, as a group or individually, must be considered power brokers because they influence the political process in every election. Part of their role during the 1992 election came in the form of a repudiation of negative advertising and campaigning, which seemed to mark the call for a new generation of politicians beginning with the Reagan election and re-election and continuing on with Bush's election in 1988. The voters proved how powerful they were in 1992 by coming out in full force to vote on election day and by being active participants during the campaign.

Conclusion

In this chapter, I have reviewed the critical forces that have altered the shape of the political campaign process. The forces include technology, structural shifts in the political process, and the shifts in influence among the power brokers. It is the power brokers who control the political process and bear the responsibility for the direction the political process takes.

Whereas the first section of the book described the transformation of marketing into the political process, the next section of the book documents how marketing was actually used by Clinton to win the White House. Concurrent to this discussion will be the assessment of the failed attempts of both Bush and Perot to rely on the same techniques.

Notes

1. Luntz (1988), p. 203.
2. Luntz (1988), p. 206.
3. Luntz (1988), p. 208.
4. Kraus (1990), p. 149.
5. Abramson, Arterton, & Orren (1988), p. 122.
6. Abramson et al., p. 122.
7. Godwin (1988), p. 1.
8. Shani & Chalasani (1992), pp. 33-42.
9. Cook (1992), p. 1.
10. Cook (1992), p. 10.
11. *The New York Times* (1992, February 21).
12. *The New York Times* (1992, April 7).
13. *The New York Times* (1992, May 14).
14. Euchner & Maltese (1992), p. 287.
15. Jamieson (1992), p. 417.
16. Pika, Mosley, & Watson (1992), p. 23.
17. Pika et al. (1992), p. 24.
18. *The New York Times* (1992, April 21).
19. Luntz (1988), p. 42.
20. Luntz (1988), p. 6.
21. Cantril (1991), p. 1.
22. Cantril (1991), p. 17.
23. McCombs, Einsiedel, & Weaver (1991), p. 95.
24. Pomper (1988), p. 282.
25. McCubbins (1992), p. 1.
26. Luntz (1988), p. 115.
27. Polsby (1980), p. 1.
28. Cantril (1991), p. 7.

PART II

The Marketing Campaign

The marketing campaign revolves around the implementation of some of the most standard marketing tools that have been used by companies to market all types of products and services. The reason for using these tools has been established in the prior chapters, and each of the environmental forces influences and affects the tools that will be described in the following chapters. There are forces in the environment that have necessitated reliance on these tools, which when used in a coordinated manner provide the candidate with the means to compete more effectively. Like companies in the commercial marketplace, campaign organizations are forced to rely on these same tools because of competitive pressures.

As mentioned earlier in the book, one of the key significant differences between political and commercial marketing is the philosophy behind the organization using the tools. Unlike a business, a political organization is driven not by profit but by a desire to implement a political ideology and approach to running the government. This by definition reflects political philosophies that drive the candidacy of the person running for office.

A second difference is timing. Everything that happens in a political campaign takes place at a faster pace than we find happening in the commercial marketplace. Marketing research, polls, and commercials are all produced under tremendous time pressures. As a result, the decision-making areas described in the following chapters have unique characteristics found only in political campaigns. They do, however, cover the same domains as we find in the commercial marketplace.

The 1992 election showcased key personalities who took the reins of control and, as in past elections, masterminded the winning strategy. The strategy that was used to win the presidency for Clinton was different than the one used to win it for Reagan and Bush in previous years. This is the result of the environmental forces previously outlined.

Clinton's people came into this election determined not to reexperience what was done to Dukakis four years ago by not responding to charges made against him. This overall strategy was epitomized at a breakfast with journalists in Washington at which Bill and Hillary Clinton showed up as a way of letting the press know that rumors about Bill's female liaisons were not of relevance now and that he and Hillary had overcome whatever marital difficulties they had in the past.

However, the breakfast meeting was hardly the end of the rumors or sensationalism that dogged Clinton for most of the campaign. The real genius in dealing with the various crises that arose, including the draft and marijuana issues, was James Carville, who reasoned that Clinton's ability to keep the agenda on the economy and off of his character would prove to be the winning formula in the election. This overall strategy was refined and honed in the summer months before the Democratic convention and was due in large part to little hope of an economic turnaround and recovery by November.

In Part II, I present a detailed analysis of the 1992 presidential campaign to cover each of the major decision-making areas that are used in a marketing campaign, whether for a product or a service: market segmentation, product positioning, and strategy formulation and imple-mentation. The analysis that follows gives a detailed account of how Clinton went about implementing his successful marketing campaign.

★4★

Voter Segmentation

At the heart of a marketing campaign is the candidates' realization that they will not be able to appeal to all voters of every persuasion. Consequently, candidates need to identify who their constituency is as they proceed through each stage of the political campaign. There is nothing new in politics about the idea of breaking down the electorate into distinct voter blocs and then creating a campaign platform that appeals to the candidate's following. Party affiliation is a concept that corresponds to this thinking; candidates build campaign platforms to advocate the issues and policies important to voters in their respective parties. New, however, is the fragmentation of the electorate, which is composed of many different voter groups, each with its own agenda (see Figure 4.1). Add to this the impact of interest groups and political action committees spending large sums of money to influence

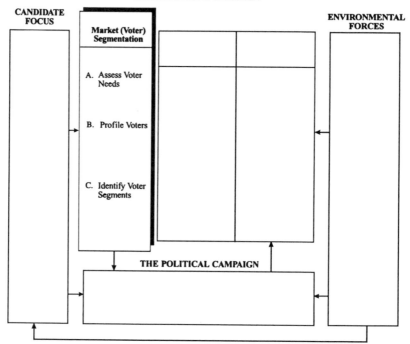

Figure 4.1. Market (Voter) Segmentation in the Model of Political Marketing

candidates' positions on issues, and candidates can no longer rely on party affiliation alone to win office.

In the commercial marketplace, marketers rely on a tool called "market segmentation" to deal with the reality of diverse and changing consumer tastes and desires. Used in connection with advances in information technology, the market segmentation tool has the ability to break a market down into distinct segments, or groups of consumers. Market segmentation analysis is used because marketers realize that their products and services cannot satisfy all consumers, and they must therefore develop products for consumers likely to buy them; products must be targeted to meet the needs and wants of specific segments of consumers. This is especially true for companies trying to compete with the powerhouses in their industry. In the soda industry, the Seven-Up company realized that its product could not compete head on with Coca-Cola and Pepsi-Cola and, as a result, called their soft drink the "Un-cola" as a way of segmenting their market.

Likewise, politicians have begun to rely on the same tool to segment groups of voters: Each segment represents a section of the electorate that will be needed to win the election. In this chapter, I will describe the market segmentation process that was used by each of the candidates running for president. The first step, using a consumer orientation, begins with an analysis of the market. Several strategic decisions will be based on this information, including the candidate's image, campaign platform, and marketing strategy.

Markets consist of buyers who are likely to differ in some way, creating the opportunity for marketers to segment a market. A commercial market can be segmented in a number of different ways. Standard segmentation strategies include breaking a market down according to geographical areas, demographic makeup, lifestyle differences, usage patterns, and attitudes, among others.

Once the segmentation strategy has been decided on, marketers then engage in what is referred to as "target marketing." According to Kotler,

> Target marketing is the decision to distinguish the different groups that make up a market and to develop appropriate product and marketing mixes for each target market. The key step in target marketing is market segmentation, which is the act of dividing a market into distinct and meaningful groups of buyers who might merit separate products and or marketing mixes. Market segmentation is a creative act.[1]

There are some basic requirements for segmenting a market in the commercial marketplace that apply to the political marketplace as well. These include three criteria: sizability, identifiability, and reachability. The use of each of these criteria rests on the logic that a market must be big enough to be profitable, and at the same time the marketer must be able to identify who the consumers are in order to reach them with their message.

A Comparison of Voter Needs and Consumer Needs

Inherent in the market segmentation process is the identification of voter needs as the initial step in dividing a market into segments. Candidates, like companies, must appeal to their constituency through the outlets available to them. Outlets such as cable television, for example, can be used to appeal to specific audiences, like those that watch C-Span and other news stations that attract "political junkies." As mentioned previously, voters have become more sophisticated and educated in their approaches to politics, as have workers in the media who cover the elections. Appealing to voters directly has become more difficult because there are lobbies and political action committees that represent the voters' special interests. These special interest groups then let the candidates know that if they do not support specific issues and policies they will not receive endorsement.

Because of the impact of television, candidates have both the opportunity and the ability to appeal to voters on many different levels, much like marketers of products and services can appeal to consumers on many different levels. There are, however, important distinctions between voters and consumers. Although the argument has been forwarded that voters are in fact consumers of a special kind, it is equally important to point out how they are different.

Voters and consumers differ across several dimensions that make segmenting a voter market a different kind of task from segmenting a consumer market. First, there are the hurdles for the candidate, namely, persuading party officials and top consultants to support him. This may involve an initial informal segmentation of this market and development of a philosophy and platform that will be attractive to this audience. This process begins well before the first primary in settings that often include party functions, at which prospective nominees are asked to make presentations before groups of influential members.

The next hurdle is the primary season, in which the candidate's challenge is to attract highly involved voters who are likely to be interested in a different set of issues than the general election voters are. To further complicate matters, the candidate must move from the primary to the convention to the general election and, at each juncture, alter his segmentation strategy to appeal to a broadening audience. In effect, the candidate is confronted with the task of appealing to the same voters with different appeals, as he moves from the primaries to the general election, and then to different voters with the same appeals, once he is in the general election. This is why segmentation is referred to as more an art than a science.

A Model of Voter Behavior

There are five components in the model used to study voters. Once the voters' motives are identified, the electorate can be broken down into segments corresponding to one or more of these five dimensions. The model is used as a substitute for party affiliation to break down the electorate into more than the usual two basic segments, Republicans and Democrats. However, the model does have a component that incorporates party affiliation into it. Because the model has also been used to identify consumer motivations in the commercial marketplace, analogies to consumers will be made as each of the five components in the model is discussed.[2]

The first component in the model is called "functional value" and represents the utility or benefit the voter expects to receive from the candidate once he takes office. Voters chose among the presidential candidates in 1992 on the basis of the issues they advocated. Clinton talked about the economy, health care coverage for all citizens, and putting people back to work, whereas Bush talked about his foreign policy accomplishments and Perot's key issues were cutting the deficit and allowing the people to take back their country. By advocating different issues and policies, each of the candidates was appealing to the American people in different ways.

This is similar to the automobile market, where one consumer segment may consider buying a Volvo because it is durable, well constructed, and safe and at the same time may consider buying a Toyota because it has better performance and a higher resale value. Here, two different automobile manufacturers focus on the same segment of consumers with different products that stress different features. In this dimension the rationally driven consumer seeks out the alternative that brings him or her the most utility.

A closer look at the issues that dominated the campaign reveals the critical differences between the three candidates across several issues, with the most pertinent issues covering the economy, taxes, the deficit, and health care. Bush's suggestions for economic changes included creating enterprise zones in inner cities and rural areas and cutting capital gains tax. Clinton talked about working with Congress to pass a jobs program as a first priority as well as increasing spending on the infrastructure. And Perot promised to establish task forces on small business and rebuild the job base through investment in the infrastructure. Regarding tax issues, Bush said he would cut taxes and balance the budget with reductions in government spending. Clinton, on the other hand, promised to increase taxes for those making over $200,000 a year, while Perot said he would tax the Social Security benefits of wealthy retirees.

Addressing the deficit, Bush said he would cap growth of entitlement programs, with the exception of Social Security. Clinton said he would balance deficit reduction with investments for economic growth. Although Perot was vague on the subject, he did promise to make deficit reduction his number one priority. Finally, focusing on health care issues, Bush promised to provide tax incentives to help uninsured citizens voluntarily buy private coverage, whereas Clinton said he would require all employers to offer coverage or pay premiums into state plans to buy private coverage for workers. Perot said he would seek a consensus on public-private effort to determine a basic benefits package for universal coverage.

Examination of the differences between each of the candidates reveals some significant divergences between their programs that had serious implications for various segments of voters. The impact on who was targeted with each of the candidates' programs will be studied later in the chapter in the analysis of the political campaign.

The second component in the model is "social value," in which the candidate is stereotyped in order to create stronger associations between the candidate and selected segments of voters in society (e.g., the perceived support of Bush by conservatives, business leaders, and the moral majority as opposed to the perceived support of Clinton by moderates, environmentalists, young voters, and gay and lesbian voters). Stereotypes are acquired by the candidate in multiple ways, including the use of selected appeals in commercials and personal endorsements of the candidate by groups or individuals or as a result of the underlying philosophy espoused by the candidate. The candidate's image is very closely connected to this component and is perhaps most affected by the candidate's membership in a political party.

The analogy to the consumer marketplace is best described in terms of the promotion of products by superstars. For example, Michael Jordan is hired by companies to endorse products in the hope that consumers will buy their products simply because they idolize him. Similarly, a candidate's association with various segments of voters creates both positive and negative images for him. For example, Clinton's vocal support of gays and lesbians created a positive image for him with the more liberal voters but a negative image for him with those who lean to the right within the Republican party.

Social value was important to Clinton's successful campaign in large part because he positioned himself as a candidate of the people. By doing this, he was able to attract voters because the leaders of more liberal groups were making public endorsements for him on television. Many voters often give their vote to a candidate without knowledge of specific issues he advocates and only on the basis of the candidate's group membership. For example, there will still be voters who cast a ballot solely on the basis of party affiliation.

Even though I have argued that the influence of the political party on candidates has diminished, it still serves as one of the most important, if not the most important, influences on a voter's choice. Thus the social value dimension incorporates the influence of party affiliation.

The third component in the model is "emotional value," which also involves the use of imagery by the candidate but in a slightly different way. In this dimension, the candidate emphasizes his personality traits to reinforce an image in the voter's mind and, by so doing, makes an emotional connection with the voter. Voters are targeted with an appeal that is linked to the sheer power of a candidate's personality, such as Perot's claim that he would be a hands-on leader based on his success and experience in the business world. Likewise, Perot used this device to differentiate himself from his opponents by asking the American voters who they would want to lend their money to. The question was framed to play on the trust issue and suggested that Perot was trustworthy whereas his opponents were not.

The candidates presented different sides of their personalities in their effort to craft a successful image for themselves. Bush wanted to be seen as the family man and a warm and caring individual who wanted a kinder, gentler nation. Bush emphasized his foreign policy experience as a way of making voters feel more secure about him. Clinton presented himself as a tenacious governor who cares about the problems of average citizens. Finally, Perot was the candidate who would tell it as it is, strong enough with his no-nonsense style to prescribe the medicine needed in this country to fix our problems.

The successful marketing of a product is often the result of stimulating emotional arousal in the consumer to trigger the purchase of a particular brand. For example, the purchase of a BMW may be triggered by the excitement one gets when sitting behind the wheel in this car. The feeling of exhilaration generated by the BMW is the result of social stereotyping used in the commercials as well as by the engineering of the car itself. BMW successfully creates this emotion by using young successful professionals in their commercials. Likewise, candidates create an emotional connection to voters by aligning themselves with other "heroes." The constant association made between Clinton and John Kennedy reinforced Clinton's image as a strong leader who represented change.

Candidates also play on voter-consumers' emotions by using the right setting and background in a commercial to create a certain mood. Bush's commercials in 1988 and Reagan's commercials in 1984 and 1980 masterfully portrayed young, flag-waving Americans to evoke patriotic emotions. This type of promotion was used to a lesser extent in 1992, although some commercials showed Bush standing next to leaders from other countries to reinforce an image of him as a world leader. In a similar way, Clinton and Gore generated images of themselves as ordinary people by surrounding themselves with average-looking voters while on their bus trips in small towns around America.

The fourth component is "conditional value," which represents the reality that sometimes a voter's choice is contingent on temporary events either in the personal life of the candidate, in the country, or perhaps in the world. A candidate's opponents often use this component as a means of creating the illusion that one candidate is better able to deal with certain crises than the other candidate (e.g., the perception that Bush would be better able to deal with Iraq and other international crises or Clinton's perceived ability to turn the economy around, given the current forces that are shaping it). This targeting device is a very effective one and incorporates the subtle and not so subtle attempts to portray one's opponents in negative terms.

Marketers use this component as the basis for appealing to consumers in a wide variety of ways. For example, companies that sell house alarms will depict situations in commercials that induce the consumers to buy alarms because the consumers imagine those events as happening to them. Another example is the plethora of recent advertisements that tell homeowners to refinance because of the inevitability that interest rates are going to rise.

Clinton won the election in 1992 in large part because of the poor state of the economy and his ability to convince voters that he could repair the country's problems. Bush tried unsuccessfully to convince voters that he was the "steady hand" in a time of crisis and that Clinton did not have the experience to make difficult decisions.

Here the candidate builds an image not on the basis of specific issues or policies he advocates but on the basis of a hypothetical situation in the mind of the voter that makes him or her think, "But what if this did happen?" By presenting hypotheticals, the candidate forces voters to make a determination in their minds on the basis of future events. The candidate who is more successful at convincing the voter that his vision of the future is the most accurate leads voters to look for qualities and campaign platforms that portray the most likely scenarios.

The fifth and final component is "epistemic value," which represents the dimension of a candidate's strategy that appeals to a voter's sense of curiosity or novelty. This device highlights voter dissatisfaction with the current administration or plays on voters' desires to see someone enter the White House who brings with him a different orientation.

Epistemic value is used in the commercial marketplace to build a marketing campaign for innovations. For example, companies sell cellular telephones by appealing to consumers' desires to acquire the latest and newest technological advances in this area. Similarly, products like Silly Putty, the Pet Rock, or the Chia Pet are promoted as novelty items that appeal to consumers' desires to have the latest fad items. Other examples abound here, such as the marketing of "Billy Beer" (the beer that Jimmy Carter's late brother Billy marketed while Carter was in the White House) on the basis of its novelty attraction. Of consumers who actually did buy a six-pack of Billy Beer, most only tried it once: There is rarely a repeat purchase of the product if it is bought solely because of its novelty. Or in the case of a candidate's election to office, voters may choose a candidate on this basis of value one time only, as was the case for Jimmy Carter in 1976.

Epistemic value was a clearly dominating force in the 1992 election, with both Clinton and Perot establishing their candidacies on the basis of change that was tied in to the poor state of the economy and the need for new leadership in Washington. Clinton was to a certain extent a curiosity factor in the minds of some voters because of his image and campaign platform that he advocated.

The Market Segmentation Strategies of Bush, Clinton, and Perot

How did each of the candidates segment their markets, that is, actually break down the market into distinct and separate segments that were important to them? Figure 4.2 is a graphic representation of four of the more visible and important voter segments that Clinton targeted with his marketing strategy.

This analysis of the market segmentation strategies of the candidates is divided into four stages: the preprimary stage, the primary stage, the convention stage, and the general election stage. Each of these stages represents major junctures in the political campaign and will set the stage for our analysis in the following two chapters.

The Preprimary Stage

One objective for a candidate in the preprimary stage is to be taken seriously by the news media. This usually means that the candidate should have won a major election for public office. In addition, the news media pay

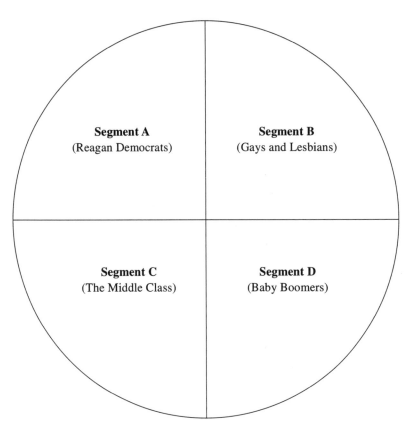

Figure 4.2. Market (Voter) Segmentation: Breaking Down the Market Into Segments
NOTE: Market segmentation is a process in which groups of voters are identified and targeted with specific appeals. Four important segments are identified here.

close attention to the fact that political consultants and staff are hired by the candidate. When the news media see this happening, they in turn make the formal declaration in the news that Candidate X is to be taken seriously.[3]

Before the primary season begins candidates organize their presentation tactics in order to maintain a certain level of visibility. Investing a significant amount of time in preprimary events, the candidates raise funds and visit states that will select delegates early in the process. During this period, the candidates must be certain that they are ideologically positioned for the primary voter, who is different from the average general election voter. A much smaller percentage of citizens vote during a primary, and those who do tend to be more interested in and concerned about politics. As a result, the candidates must introduce different appeals during the primaries than during the general election.[4]

Since Reagan built up his new coalition of voters, several regional changes have taken place, the most noteworthy of which is in the South, a segment loyal to Republican candidates since 1980. Bush attempted to hold on to the Reagan coalition but was not able to in large part because of Pat Buchanan's challenge. Buchanan appealed to the extreme right and in effect was able to siphon off his support from those voters. The voters loyal to Buchanan had strong views on affirmative action and welfare and supported Buchanan's call for trade barriers that would keep immigrants from third world countries out of the United States.[5]

Bush expected the challenge from Buchanan on the right but never expected he would form such a formidable following. Before the primaries began, Bush started out his re-election bid with a promise to the American voters that he would fix what was causing the sluggish economy and introduced some measures to that end. In effect, Bush was targeting the constituency that put him into office. This was not enough, however. Perhaps Bush's biggest problems were overestimating his own popularity and overdepending on the support that the Iraqi victory could afford him. Bush used Congress and the Federal Reserve Board as scapegoats and thus cushioned himself in a sense of security. But, ultimately, the lack of a strong enough recovery hurt Bush. The statistics on the economy simply did not support his campaign assertion that the economy was recovering, at least not fast enough to suit many of the unemployed workers.[6]

Bush's nosedive in the polls was stunning but reflected his inability to find the right message to use to appeal to his market of voters. The summer before the primaries began, Bush was at his peak in the polls. Bush's strategy at that point had been to appeal to voters' emotional values and to position himself as a war hero as well as a decisive and strong leader. However, that appeal was dropped as voters became more concerned with functional values and, specifically, with their pocketbooks. Around Labor Day, the Misery Index (a combination of inflation and unemployment rates) revealed a strong lack of confidence in the economy, and, as a result, the economy began to dominate campaign issues. Bush then tried to respond as best he could with new proposals.[7]

At this stage in the campaign, several Democrats declared candidacy, none of whom included any of the better-known Washington politicians. Richard Gephardt, Sam Nunn, Al Gore, and some other potential candidates decided not to run for the White House against a sitting president who looked invincible. But, of the Democrats who did declare, it soon became apparent that Clinton was the best organized. Perot was not a familiar name to most Americans at this stage in the campaign.

The Primary Stage

During this stage, it is critical for the candidate to try to manipulate the mass media's reporting focus. The candidate must particularly try to have some impact on the before-and-after reporting of the primary elections, especially concerning who won and who lost, which is sometimes called the "expectations game." The candidates engage in spin control, that is, control over the version of the story the candidates and their handlers like to give to the media, or the so-called spin they put on the information. Interpretation of the primary results is as important as or more important than the actual outcome. The candidate who loses but does better than expected may in fact be the bigger winner than the one who wins but falls below expectations. It is, therefore, to the advantage of a candidate to hold his pre-election claims to a minimum.[8]

Primaries have major effects on candidates and their strategies because they compel candidates to raise money so that they establish credibility early in the process. Therefore the most important aspect of the primaries is how they are analyzed in relation to their effect on public opinion and, in turn, how this information is mediated by the press. In addition, the rules of the major parties for counting primary votes makes a significant difference to the development of strategy. The results of early polls and primaries are covered extensively by the press, which creates pressure on party leaders to commit themselves quickly to the front-runner. Primaries are also important because most delegates are selected during that time. Because the results represent an objective indication of whether a candidate can win the general election, the primaries also affect donations of money from interest groups and political action committees.[9]

The primaries are to a politician what test markets are to a marketer. In a test market, a company offers a product to a carefully selected audience for a limited period of time. The audience is selected to mirror the characteristics of the whole market. For example, if a company wants to market a product around the whole country, it may choose Peoria as a test market site because the demographic characteristics and consumption patterns of the people that live there closely resemble the makeup of the whole country. The product is offered only for a limited period of time to determine how well it would fare in the rest of the country.

Primaries serve in the same capacity for candidates, who use them to test various appeals to determine which candidate image and issues are the most attractive to voters in the various states where the primaries are held. There is no doubt that voters in New Hampshire, hit very hard by the poor economic conditions at the time of the election, would have different concerns than voters in Chicago, who were not hit as hard.

Clinton started out poorly in New Hampshire largely because of his bad publicity; instead of communicating his message of change and economic reform, he was forced to defend himself constantly on several fronts. The media were more interested in talking about his character than his campaign platform. Some argued that this was done because it made for good news, whereas others argued that character is the most important ingredient to leadership and should therefore be explored in its entirety. Thus the challenge to the Clinton organization was how to change the focus of the media. The Clinton organizers were sure that once his message got out his ratings in the polls would improve.

However, even with all his bad publicity, Clinton placed second in the New Hampshire primary and won the expectations game. For Clinton to have come in second meant that he made a tremendous comeback and had momentum on his side. Clinton came across as a fighter; when he appeared on several television interview programs during the last week of the primary, he did very well. Some within his campaign thought he had acquired the status of a celebrity, which meant he would be accepted, flaws and all.[10]

When Clinton began to appeal to voters on an emotional dimension, not only their hearts but also their minds opened up to allow his message about change and the economy to filter through. Clinton's main rival in the early primaries was Paul Tsongas, who appealed to the well-educated and higher-income voters who were looking for a candidate with a pro-business posture.[11] The profile of the typical Tsongas voter was young and conservative on economic issues but socially liberal. Clinton took advantage of this by trying to stereotype Tsongas as a candidate who walked, talked, and looked like a Democrat but thought like a Republican.[12] His other major opponent during the primaries was Jerry Brown, whose loyal segment of voters was very supportive of his call for sweeping changes in the national health care system.

The most important focus of Clinton's segmentation strategy during the primaries centered on a key segment of voters, namely, the middle class. This was the ultimate market segment (considered to be 63% of the American population) that, because of the policies of the last decade, was feeling the brunt of the economy's downturn. Each of the candidates running in the primaries was appealing to this segment in a slightly different way.

Paul Tsongas repeatedly said that he was not Santa Claus to emphasize that it would take hardship on the part of everyone to correct the economic problems facing the country. Brown played on the middle-class segment's dissatisfaction with the economy and tried to broaden it into a disgust with the entire system of government in Washington.[13] In addition, Brown tried to extend his base of support by announcing very early on that Jesse Jackson would be his choice for vice president, thereby appealing to voters by stereotyping himself through his association with Jackson.[14]

There was another key market segment that Clinton knew he had to win over if he wanted to win the White House, namely, the Southern voters. By sweeping the primaries in the South and following that victory with a win in the Midwest, Clinton would have secured the nomination. However, he still had to fight off a determined Brown in the New York and California primaries. Brown's strategy was to do enough damage to Clinton to in turn attract some of the "Washington insiders" to enter the race. That strategy never worked because voters in these and other primaries began to take a closer look at Brown's flat tax, considered to be off-the-wall by many voters and opinion leaders in the media.[15]

The real story during the primaries was on the Democratic side of the fence. Although Bush had his hands full with Pat Buchanan during the primaries, Bush eventually fought off Buchanan's challenge. Buchanan built up his base of power with the voters during the primaries to set the stage for his best punch, which was not delivered until the convention.

The Convention Stage

Ross Perot changed the usual formula in politics about the time the convention rolled around. Nominations are usually wrapped up before the convention convenes, with little room for outsiders to alter this calculus. However, Perot changed this; he was the first to enter at this stage as a dark horse in over 30 years.

The convention is a meeting in which the candidates and their chief supporters try to maintain their communications with as many delegates as they can. By the time of the nominating convention, most delegates are already pledged to a candidate, and a probable winner has emerged. The convention merely ratifies the result.[16]

Both Clinton and Bush confronted a new threat as the conventions approached. Even though each had wrapped up his respective nominations, Perot had captured the imagination and curiosity of the media and voters. Not the typical, run-of-the-mill politician, Perot was the "unpolitician" (à la "Uncola"), that is, everything a politician was not supposed to be in this modern age of politics. He professed to having no spin doctors or handlers. His image was multifaceted and spoke to voters' patriotism, desire for change, and hopes that the American dream could be there for their children and grandchildren. Perot appealed to several different segments of voters with his message.[17]

Perot began to receive so much media attention that the Clinton campaign became concerned, especially when their candidate's ratings in the polls plummeted to third place by early June.[18] Clinton responded by issuing a new economic plan, titled "Putting People First." Along with his new plan, Clinton brought out the contrast between his specifics and Perot's vagueness. Perhaps Perot's biggest mistake was not issuing his plan sooner: His plan appeared after he dropped out of the race in July.

At the Democratic convention, Clinton reached out to another key voter segment, the support of which he knew he needed to win, namely, the Reagan Democrats. The Reagan Democrats—those Democrats who had defected to Reagan—were feeling the pinch of the economy, and Clinton promised he would look out for them in his administration.[19] Carville, Clinton's top strategist, believed that the addition of Gore in mid-June was the turning point in the campaign. According to his thinking, the addition of Gore changed the way voters perceived Clinton.[20]

At the Republican convention, there were attacks on some segments of voters that fatally damaged Bush's image. Beginning with a speech on prime time television by Pat Buchanan, there was continued wholesale bashing of homosexuals and constant reference to family values during the convention. The Republicans wanted to advertise the fact that, in their words, Clinton was giving special treatment to the lesbian and gay segments of voters. This led to further debate at the convention on the treatment of AIDS, an issue closely tied to these segments of voters.[21] The state of the Republican party after the convention was a disaster, and not even Jim Baker could pull them out this time.

It was a tumultuous time for Perot as well, who entered, left, and then reentered the race. Perot's proposals, however, hit several voter segments, increasing his appeal. He called for higher income taxes for the wealthy; increased gasoline taxes, which would affect just about everyone who drives; investment in education, which would affect the whole public school system; and a very controversial program to tax Social Security beneficiaries. Perot's whole program revolved around reducing the budget deficit, which had a very strong appeal to middle-class voters who knew something had to be done about the deficit to take the pressure off of them.[22]

The General Election Stage

Once the convention is over, campaigning for the general election officially begins, and workers must be activated by giving them purpose. A second task is generating positive media coverage. The sheer size of the electorate and the fact that many, if not most, voters get their information from television together mean that the media have become more important in the election process. For the vast majority of citizens in America, campaigns do not function so much to change minds as to reinforce their previous attitudes and behaviors. The challenge to Democrats is to get the voters to turn out to vote, because they have a majority of voters loyal to their party; because more Republicans actually vote, most important to them is party identification.[23]

Clinton's success in the general election can be attributed to several factors, but perhaps the most important was the centrist approach of his economic program. With this message, he segmented his market on a very broad basis, appealing to segments with a moderate as opposed to liberal appeal. He also planned well not only before the primaries began but even while in office as governor. Finally, his ability to withstand with grace the constant pressure from the media reinforced his image as a strong leader.[24]

The bus trip around the country with Gore strengthened the image that Clinton was just an ordinary guy. It was the reincarnation of the Truman Whistle Stop train ride and reinforced Clinton's theme, "Putting People First." It is interesting to note that the idea for the bus trip was a reaction to Dukakis's failed strategy of 4 years earlier, when he came out of the convention with an impressive lead but lost momentum because he stopped campaigning until Labor Day. Clever about the bus trips was the idea of giving the local reporters and journalists who could not afford to travel by plane the opportunity to meet the presidential candidate. The net impact of this strategy was more media attention around the country.[25]

In a postelection interview with Clinton's top advisers, Stan Greenberg, Clinton's pollster, talked about how the candidate had successfully reached out to the old Reagan coalition, which he believed collapsed with this election. This included the young voters, business people, entrepreneurs, and others often referred to as the Reagan Democrats. Bush won in 1988 by hanging on to this critical coalition but lost in 1992 because of the defection of one half of these voters. Clinton reached into several market segments previously loyal to Reagan and Bush, including voters over the age of 65, voters under the age of 30, Southerners, suburbanites, Western voters, and the very large and important segment of middle-class voters. Clinton accomplished this with a message that let these voters think of themselves as "New Democrats" or moderates. According to Greenberg, just as there was a Reagan era, there will be a Clinton era.[26]

In August 1992, while Clinton was riding around the country in a bus with Gore, Bush was wasting this crucial time. Bush got a late start, and his campaign organization was disorganized until Baker became involved. Then Bush stepped up his attack on Clinton and Gore by trying to stereotype them in the most negative way possible. He labeled them as environmental extremists and warned that their policies would leave hundreds of thousands of automobile workers out of jobs. Bush continued to appeal to voters by referring to his victory in the Iraqi war but apparently to no avail. Bush's appeal revolved around the claim that America needed a leader who was stable and that if a crisis were to arise he would be the best candidate to handle it.[27]

Meanwhile, Perot was introducing the American electorate to a new form of campaigning by debuting the "infomercial," clearly an appeal to the functional side of voters who wanted to know how he was going to fix the economy. Using pie charts and diagrams, Perot reached out to segments of voters who were dissatisfied with the way things were run in Washington, DC. His campaign was built in large part on his ability to tap into voters' desire for change and his representation of a very different style to government than what Clinton and Bush were offering the American people.

In his book *United We Stand*, Perot gave some specifics of his economic plan—such as raising the gasoline tax to 50 cents per gallon, raising the top income tax rate to 33%, and taking 10% out of spending for many pro-grams—that turned off many voter segments. However, his way of address-ing the concerns of a broad base of voters was to argue that he could reduce the budget deficit and balance the budget in 5 years.[28]

Conclusion

In politics, the importance of assessing voters' needs and understanding what motivates them could very well decide the difference between winning and losing. Candidates use market segmentation analysis to break voters down into different segments. Each segment is then identified according to the unique needs that separate it from others. I discussed how each of the three presidential candidates segmented his markets at each stage of the political campaign. The segmentation of the electorate served as the foundation on which the candidates developed their respective positioning and marketing strategies.

By the time the general election rolls around, there are so many distinct and different segments of voters that the successful candidate must reach out to the voters loyal to his opponents in order to win. A candidate's market seg-mentation strategy broadens to a point at which the candidates have to worry less about appealing to specific segments, as they did during the primaries and convention, and target a broader appeal to all segments. The successful segmentation strategy is one that conveys an image that incorporates all of the specifics of the candidate's platform yet is unique enough to distinguish him from his opponents. This is referred to as a candidate's "positioning strategy," a concept that will be discussed in detail in the next chapter on candidate positioning.

Notes

1. Kotler (1982), p. 217.
2. Sheth, Newman, & Gross (1991), p. 7. The model was applied to political settings in Newman & Sheth (1987), p. 31.
3. Polsby (1980), p. 88.
4. Polsby (1980), p. 88.
5. *U.S. News and World Report* (1992, September 23).
6. *Newsweek* (1992, October 21), p. 54.
7. *Time* (1992, November 2), p. 29.

8. Polsby (1980), p. 92.

9. Polsby (1980), p. 92.

10. *The New York Times* (1992, February 21).

11. *The New York Times* (1992, February 27).

12. *The New York Times* (1992, February 27).

13. *Time* (1992, March 2), p. 17.

14. *The New York Times* (1992, March 23).

15. *Time* (1992, November 2), p. 28.

16. Polsby (1980), p. 115.

17. *The New York Times* (1992, July 9).

18. *Time* (1992, November 2), p. 28.

19. *The New York Times* (1992, August 20).

20. Clinton/Gore campaign (1992).

21. *The New York Times* (1992, August 20).

22. *The New York Times* (1992, July 21).

23. Polsby (1980), p. 156.

24. *Time* (1992, November 2), p. 29.

25. *Time* (1992, November 2), p. 29.

26. Clinton/Gore campaign (1992).

27. *Time* (1992, November 2), p. 29.

28. *Time* (1992, October 12), p. 38.

★5★

Candidate Positioning

A candidate must have a clear focus on who he is and what he stands for if the vision he presents to the American people is going to be effectively communicated. Positioning is a marketing tool that captures the essence of a candidate's vision and structures strategy. The actual process of developing the candidate's position involves several steps. First, there must be an assessment of the candidate's own strengths and weaknesses, resulting in the articulation of his political philosophy. Next, the same process must be carried out for the candidate's opposition to provide insight into the competitive environment within which the candidate will be operating. The candidate must then target selected segments of voters toward whom he will direct his appeals, a process that cannot be completed until the candidate has a firm grasp of the philosophical differences between him and his opponents.

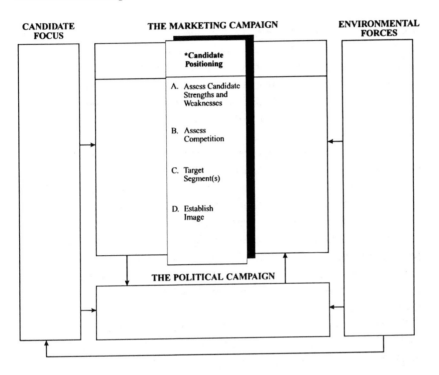

Figure 5.1. The Role of Candidate Positioning in the Model of Political Marketing

The outcome of this process is the establishment of the candidate's image or the picture in voters' minds of who the candidate is and what he stands for. The candidate's image then becomes the strategic focus of his marketing strategy. In this chapter, I will analyze how the 1992 presidential candidates positioned themselves (see Figure 5.1).

In the commercial marketplace, cigarette ads emphasizing the cowboy image associated with smoking Marlboros, for example, would be targeted at consumers who want to feel macho. That consumer would probably be a male individual, proud of his masculinity, who wants to project a tough demeanor to others. This could include truck drivers, young male teenagers, and anyone else who is depicted in the research as a likely candidate for smoking this brand of cigarettes.

Why do marketers engage in this activity? The answer is simple and at the same time critical to the success of product sales. The main reason for positioning is to make the best use of a marketer's resources. For example, it does not make sense to advertise Marlboros to females, who in all likelihood would not be interested in projecting a macho, cowboy image. Therefore it is vital that a marketer identify the demographic makeup of the market segments he or she has identified. Demographic breakdowns reveal media habits, which can then lead the marketer to choose the appropriate promotional outlets for appeals to consumers.

Likewise, this same analysis can be applied to political candidates. Candidates use two strategic devices to create their position in the political marketplace: (a) the campaign platform they put forward and (b) the image they create for themselves. A candidate's image is designed to be broad enough to relate to all the possible segments of voters the candidate is trying to address, and, at the same time, the image must be crafted in response to his opponents' images. The campaign platform becomes an avenue through which a candidate can offer specific policies to reinforce his image. For example, Bill Clinton reinforced his image as a leader who cares about people by calling for free immunizations for all children.

The candidates in 1992 positioned themselves very differently, each with a unique image. George Bush positioned himself as the president who would give power back to the people by reforming government and offered the voters leadership based on experience. Clinton positioned himself by saying that all Americans must give and not just receive and not just place blame but also take responsibility. Ross Perot's image centered on his motto "United We Stand" and how he would be proud to go to Washington as the servant of the people. Each of the candidates relied on sophisticated marketing research to work out the details of their positions.

Assessing the Candidate's Strengths and Weaknesses

Looking back at the 1992 election, there were several crucial tests that determined how each of the three candidates' strengths and weaknesses played with the American voter. Clinton's tests came early on in the campaign, namely, during the primary season, when voters were given the opportunity to respond to claims of Clinton's marital infidelity and draft status during the Vietnam War. Perhaps even more important than the claims about his character was his ability to respond to the accusations in a cool and collected manner, which shaped voters' perception of him as a very composed leader.

Subsequently, his positions on the issues and in particular his concern with the economy became real strengths for Clinton.

Bush's tenure in office served as the assessment period for voters' perceptions of his strengths and weaknesses. Unfortunately for him, the Iraqi war came too soon in his term and, as a result, voters began to focus on the economy and less on his accomplishments overseas by the time the election process began. Perhaps his greatest strength was his foreign policy accomplishments and his greatest weakness was his refusal to acknowledge that the country was in a recession.

Perot's strengths and weaknesses ebbed and flowed along with the ups and downs of his ratings in the polls. At first, Perot's real strength came from his outsider status and the perception that he was not a typical Washington insider who would conduct business as usual. He was credited as being a real success story because he worked to become one of the nation's richest men. His greatest strengths were his perceived ability to get things done and his representation of real change at a time when the average voter was totally dissatisfied with the status quo. Furthermore, Perot's stellar performance in the first debate sent his popularity rating soaring and proved to add strength to his candidacy. One of his greatest weaknesses, however, came when he dropped out of the race while at or near the top of the polls. Voters saw Perot as a quitter and perhaps this more than anything else brought him back into the race. However, claims emerged that he carried out investigations on some of the volunteers working for him. His popularity declined rapidly after the *60 Minutes* interview in which he specifically accused the Bush organization of dirty tricks and a threat to disrupt his daughter's wedding. In the end, Perot was not perceived to be the type of leader voters wanted; he was perceived as too "thin-skinned."

Assessing Competition

Throughout the election campaign, and in the process of developing the candidate's own position, competitors' strengths and weaknesses must be constantly monitored. Perhaps it is important at this point to define what strengths and weaknesses are. Here, the polls once again become crucial to the success of the candidate. This is also where marketing research and polling are best distinguished. Marketing research is used to determine why voters prefer or dislike a candidate, and polling is used to monitor the candidate's standing in the minds of voters with respect to the candidate's characteristics. If a candidate is doing well in the polls, he can be assured that his strengths are seen as more attractive than his competitors', or, on the other hand, that his weaknesses are not perceived to be as bad as the competition's.

When does a candidate know which of his own or his competitors' strengths are accounting for his ranking in the polls? This is where marketing research plays a crucial role and is separate from the use of focus groups. The focus groups can give a candidate only an idea of what might or might not play well with voters, whereas marketing research determines which of a candidate's strengths and weaknesses will have a direct impact on his ratings in the polls.

Targeting Segments

From a candidate's point of view, it is critical for him to remain flexible and be able to direct his appeals to those segments that will ensure him victory at each stage of the campaign. However, looking at what transpired during the 1992 campaign we see that this is easier said than done: For example, Bush unsuccessfully attempted to reposition himself after the convention. Thus another ingredient that becomes crucial to successful repositioning is the choice of a theme that attracts voters. As the campaign moved into the general election stage, Clinton's message of change in the economy became the apparent winning theme.

According to David Wilhelm, Clinton's campaign manager, the targeting strategy that won the election for Clinton was based on the division of the country into three target groups of states: the top-end states, the play hard states, and the big challenge states. The last two groups are what the Clinton campaigners referred to as their "battleground states." States were categorized into one of the three target segments using several criteria, including economic performance, presidential historical preferences, Democratic performance, the Southern factor (called "cultural affinity," representing voter attitudes toward candidates from Southern states), and constant polling. In total, 32 states were targeted and 19 states (including the District of Columbia) were not targeted. Out of the 32 states targeted (totaling 376 electoral votes), Clinton won 31 and lost only in North Carolina. Out of the 19 states that were not targeted, only one (Nevada) fell into the Clinton column.[1]

The top-end states were considered to be states that could be won with a limited allocation of resources. These states included Arkansas, Massachusetts, Rhode Island, West Virginia, Hawaii, California, and Illinois. All of these states were won by Clinton, allowing him to spend more time in the battleground states that were more competitive. In particular, the ability to place California and Illinois into this target group freed up an enormous amount of time and resources for the Clinton organization.[2]

The battleground states included the play hard states (those that both the Clinton and Bush camps went after) and the big challenge states (those that the Clinton camp did not think they could win). The most dollars and time were spent on the play hard states, every one of which Clinton won with the exception of North Carolina. These states included, among others, Maryland, Delaware, Missouri, Colorado, Pennsylvania, Georgia, Iowa, Kentucky, Louisiana, Maine, Michigan, Montana, North Carolina, New Mexico, New Jersey, Ohio, Tennessee, and Wisconsin. Clinton had a good two-week edge on Bush in these states, which allowed him to get earlier media coverage. From a targeting standpoint, the Clinton organization was very successful.[3]

Establishing Image

As pointed out before, the audience gets broader as the candidate moves from the primaries to the convention and finally to the general election. Each candidate begins with an understanding of the electorate and the segments of voters he is targeting at various times during the campaign. He next makes the necessary changes that sharpen his image to ensure victory at each stage of the campaign. This is done within the constraints of the philosophy and dictates of both the candidate and the party that he represents, but, as we have pointed out repeatedly in the book, the philosophy of the candidate (as reflected in his platform and image) is significantly influenced by the most current poll results. In addition, the party no longer has the power it formerly had and thus can no longer dictate the philosophy the candidate is espousing.

A candidate image is defined quite succinctly by Nimmo:

> To bridge the gap between what political scientists know about electoral behavior and the notion that voters are consumers, a concept called the image is used. Image consists of the person's subjective understanding of things, i.e., of what he or she believes to be true about something, likes or dislikes, about it. This

use of image parallels the definition of brand image in advertising and market research. As with brand images, political images do not exist apart from the political objects (or their symbolic surrogates) that stimulate political thoughts, feelings, and inclinations. In sum, an image is a human construct imposed upon an array of perceived attributes projected by an object, event, or person. Thus, for instance, a candidate's image consists of how voters perceive him, perceptions based upon both the subjective appraisals made by the voters and the messages (utterances, attributes, qualities, etc.) transmitted by the candidate.[4]

Clinton was successful in building an image of change that was consistently reinforced throughout the campaign. His image was supported with views on the economy and social welfare that differentiated him from his competitors throughout the political campaign. Each of the stages in the political campaign will be analyzed now in light of the positioning strategies used by each of the three candidates.

The Candidate-Positioning Strategies of Bush, Clinton, and Perot

In Figure 5.2, I illustrate the use of candidate positioning with a positioning map, a two-dimensional space that plots the positions of the candidates. This graphical representation is computer generated from a sophisticated software program that processes the results of survey research carried out with voters.[5] The map pictured here was developed by hand to illustrate the use of this technique and represents a snapshot of the candidates' positions at the end of the election. Keep in mind that positioning is a dynamic process, and a candidate's "position" is always changing throughout course of the political campaign.

Two polls conducted after the convention suggested that voters were looking for a leader who advocated strong change. In one poll conducted by *Time* magazine from August 25 to 30, 1992, results indicated that over 40% of those polled thought that the economic conditions in their part of the country were either poor or very poor.[6] In a poll reported in *USA Today* on November 4, 1992, 50% believed that Clinton could bring about the change needed for economic turnaround, 47% thought Perot could, and only 20% thought that Bush could. When voters were asked about the candidates' leadership qualities, 31% thought Bush had the right experience; 31% thought Clinton had the best plan for the country, whereas 28% sided with Perot; and only 20% thought Perot had strong convictions.[7]

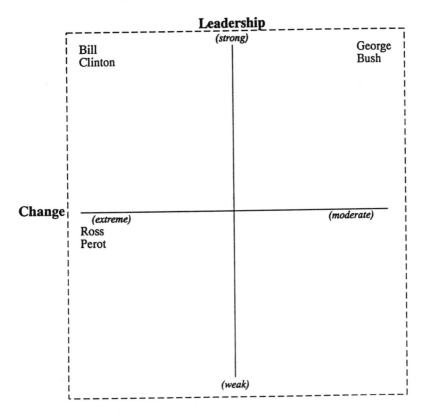

Figure 5.2. Candidate Positioning
NOTE: Candidate positioning is a strategic tool that plots the candidate's image onto a two-dimensional map.
The location of each candidate represents his position in the market.

Clinton won the election in 1992 because of his ability to position himself
as a strong leader who wanted to make drastic changes in Washington; Bush
lost because he was perceived as a strong leader who advocated only moderate
changes. Perot, however, lost because of his inability to convince the American electorate that he was a strong leader despite his advocacy of extreme
change. In the end, Americans wanted both strong leadership and drastic
changes in Washington.

The mapping process represented in Figure 5.2 is used during each stage
of the political campaign to reflect subtle changes in the candidates' positions
as their popularity ebbs and flows. As he moves through each stage of the
campaign, the candidate repositions himself in response to the growing

number of market segments he must appeal to in order to win. In effect, the candidate's position is a reflection of how voters perceive him, which is why it is important to generate the map on the basis of survey research. This tool becomes an efficient way of testing the effectiveness of a candidate's own promotional strategy as well as of determining how thorough his opponents' strategies have been. In sum, it provides an avenue for measuring how effective the candidate's attempts have been to create a specific image for himself.

The Preprimary Stage

Clinton's advantage early on in the campaign was being chosen by the media as the front-runner. Clinton appealed to the media (which have a tremendous amount of power before the primaries begin) with his personality and ideas. He immediately carved out a position for himself on the basis of the changes he proposed for the middle class. Add to that Clinton's ease with hugging a voter instead of shaking his or her hand, and the image of a likable, caring individual comes through.[8]

As the campaign moved on through the next three stages, it also became clear that the cool, calm, and collected Clinton would fight back until he beat back the charges leveled against him. It was this dimension of leadership that enabled Clinton to define a position for himself as a strong leader.

As the campaign began to take shape, Clinton's competitors influenced the shaping of his image. Jerry Brown, the only Democrat who had sought nomination before, had high name recognition. Although attractive to the voter totally dissatisfied with Washington, Brown's message and appeal did not resonate well in the ears of the mainstream voter. Harkin positioned himself based on his association with labor and traditional Democrats and his advocacy of an old-fashioned liberal program. This, however, did not work in 1992 because voters wanted change to an extent that he did not offer.[9]

Many analysts coming into the primaries thought Bob Kerrey was the man to beat because he started out his campaign with significant force. However, his leadership turned out to be hollow: He had an impressive background as a war hero, successful businessman, and former governor but could not back up his call for change in government with any specifics other than calling for a national health care program. He never came across as a strong leader. Paul Tsongas was the one candidate who really challenged Clinton and pressured him to articulate a persuasive image. As an advocate of several serious changes in government policy, Tsongas was in tune with the country's desire for change and had a plan to back it up.[10]

The problem with Bush's position at this period in the campaign revolved around his tenure in the White House, which had been without any clear vision. Many voters perceived him as a leader who would not bring about great change in his second term, and the sentiment among some was that Bush was not shaping history with his program. With the demise of communism and the Iraqi war victory to his credit, Bush was ready to rest on his laurels and hope that his successes would be enough to convince voters of his strong leadership.[11]

The Primary Stage

During the primary Clinton struggled to shift discussion away from his character to his plan of change for the economy. As the Democratic candidates jockeyed for position in the polls during the primaries, one very serious concern voiced by many voters was the electability factor. Tsongas began to be thought of as unelectable as the primaries moved into the South, where Clinton had some very impressive victories. It then became apparent that Clinton was going to be the nominee.[12]

Tsongas created his position around the image of a candidate who was sincere and moral, based in part on the ideas he advocated in a book he wrote. Brown, on the other hand, defined himself through his pledge not to accept contributions over $100. This sent a strong message to voters and allowed Brown to position himself as a candidate who repudiated the way politics operated in this country. Each of Clinton's main rivals sought to position himself in a way that would make him stand out from the crowd: Clinton with his detailed plan, Tsongas with his new ideas, and Brown with his limits on campaign contributions.[13]

On the Republican side, Pat Buchanan took advantage of his outsider status and thus tried to position himself as a populist who wanted to fight the Washington insiders.[14] Buchanan tried to bolster his outsider appeal with a pitch to buy American, and along with this theme came various issues and policies, including very strong trade barriers, that would support that view. However, his image was immediately tarnished when voters discovered that his wife drove a Mercedes Benz.

Bush was having difficulty depending solely on his reputation from the Iraqi war and realized that he had to take an offensive stance and rely on a negative campaign against the Democrats and Clinton in particular, if he was going to win a second term. Even though Bush said the personal lives of candidates were campaign taboo, he began a relentless attack on Clinton that lasted for the duration of the campaign. Using his aides to deliver the "blows," Bush positioned himself as the best leader for the country by attacking Clinton's character and policies. Bush thus made the implication that he was the preferred candidate because he did not suffer from the same problems that ailed Clinton.

Bush's personal attacks remained very harsh throughout this stage of the campaign. Bush even referred to Clinton and Gore as bimbos and clowns later on in the campaign in a last-ditch effort to do more damage to their campaign, although he probably did more damage to himself than he did to them. Bush portrayed Clinton's health care program as one that would have the compassion of the KGB, for example. The attempt to position his opponents in a negative light was a strategy that worked for Bush in 1988 but failed in 1992 in large part because the Clinton organization responded quickly and tenaciously to Bush's attacks.[15]

The Convention Stage

As Clinton came into the convention, his job was to reposition the Democratic party as one that was based on new and different ideas and to create a position for the party and himself in a much more moderate way than it had been perceived.[16] Because the market broadens as the candidates enter the convention stage, the task here is not only to appeal to loyal Democratic voters but to reach out to Republican voters. To achieve this goal, Clinton asked Al Gore to be his running mate. This unorthodox choice won immediate approval from everyone. In this case, geographical diversity did not play a role in deciding who to pick for a running mate.

The Clinton/Gore ticket was comprised of the youngest candidates to run for the White House in history. The youth of the two candidates reinforced their position during this stage as a vibrant choice for change from the old ways of running the country. In stark contrast, Bush was 68 years old and had been a Washington insider for over 2 decades.[17]

An appeal to the baby boomer generation was very evident at the convention, at which Clinton and Gore tried to appeal to these voters' desires to see their children do better economically than they did.[18] The Democratic convention served as the official beginning of an opportunity not only to define who Clinton and Gore were but also to start the attack on Bush's economic programs of the past 4 years. In addition, the convention was used to dispel any negative impressions that voters had about Clinton's character. Negative characterizations were effectively dispersed by having an emotionally charged production made of defining who Clinton was and where he came from. Many voters did not know, for example, that he grew up as a fatherless child and lived with an alcoholic stepfather.[19]

Throughout the convention, Clinton continued to talk about the middle class and the need to rescue ordinary people from the ravages of the economy. In effect, Clinton successfully positioned himself as a person who came from a very ordinary background and could relate to the hardship that average, middle-class citizens were experiencing. He came across as a very compassionate person who espoused a philosophy of new choices based on old values. Along with this theme Clinton called for all Americans to take responsibility. In terms of their convention, the Democrats were successful. The infighting of the past was gone, and Clinton and his organization felt that they had dispelled the character accusations that plagued Clinton throughout the primaries.[20] However, a new problem emerged: Perot. Perot's entrance onto the scene put Clinton into third place in the polls. Perot's strong presence threw a curve into the easy sailing that the Democrats envisioned for the rest of the campaign.

After the Democratic convention, the Republicans had their opportunity to define who they were, with Bush trying hard to project an image of himself as a strong leader. Bush tried to carve for himself a position of decisive and experienced leadership during the convention. However, this was difficult after a successful Democratic convention that placed Bush behind Clinton in the polls by approximately 20 percentage points. Realizing that Clinton had altered the focus of the campaign from his character to the economy, Bush then brought out the differences between himself and Clinton along economic policy lines.[21]

Bush had his hands full at this time in the campaign. He had alienated the right wing in the Republican party since his victory in 1988 and in this election had to contend with Buchanan and Perot. In a three-way race, Bush believed that voters would switch to Perot if they were dissatisfied with him.[22]

As a result of these mounting pressures at the convention, Bush relied on a negative attack, which turned ugly in a personal way, against Bill and Hillary Clinton. Bush tried to position Clinton as a gamble for voters, especially in light of the role that his wife might play in his administration. The Clinton camp responded vigorously and aggressively to these types of accusations, retaliating by focusing on the economy, the Republicans' weakness. Clinton pointed out that he would be his own economic czar, not deferring to someone like Jim Baker, whom Bush touted as the economic expert during the convention.[23]

Trying to develop a position for himself as just an ordinary person was difficult if not impossible for Bush. He could not escape the trappings of power in the White House. Unlike Clinton and Gore, who had taken to the small towns in America on a bus, Bush was forced to travel in the presidential jet because of the size of his entourage. The tone was set for the general election: Clinton and Gore had successfully established a position for themselves as candidates in touch with the people and ready for change, whereas Bush and Quayle remained the candidates of the past, not in tune with the mood of the country.[24]

At this period in the campaign, voters were voicing their dislike for both parties and especially with the way the process was working. Not wanting to vote for either Bush or Clinton, some voters polled were beginning to say that they would vote for Perot simply to make a statement about their discontentment with the system. The position that Perot had molded for himself was the voice for the discontented.[25]

The General Election Stage

Each of the three candidates' positions was solidified in the general election stage of the campaign. As depicted in Figure 5.2, Clinton eventually won because he was perceived as the leader who would bring about change in government, and voters thought he had the leadership qualities necessary to facilitate change. Bush lost because he was perceived as a leader who was out of touch and not ready to make the necessary changes in the country. The economic figures that came out the month before the election, indicating an economy stalled in its tracks, did a disservice to Bush, who had no defined program to remedy the situation. Perot came in a very respectable third, resting on his position as a leader who perhaps did not measure up to Bush and Clinton as a political leader but rather as a candidate who did have his finger on the pulse of the country; he understood the desire on the part of voters for some real change in this country. As we found out in the months that followed the election, Perot's message did not die with the election.

Coming into the general election, Bush defined his position as a strong leader on the basis of his foreign policy accomplishments. He continued his attack against Clinton, often comparing himself to Clinton with respect to who could best deal with a man like Saddam Hussein.[26]

In making international leadership the focus of his campaign, Bush discovered that the country was more concerned with its economic woes than its international fears. The American people realized that, without any serious plan articulated, Bush could not be the leader to deal with these issues. He simply never defined himself as a candidate who would bring about change, and it was too late for repositioning at the general election stage. If Bush were to advocate strong measures to fix the economy, he would raise the question in many voters' minds of why he waited so long to do this. On the other hand, if he acknowledged the weak economy, he would put himself in the position of criticizing his own past administration.[27]

In an effort to redefine Clinton's image, Bush used a strategy known as attack and apologize. As its name suggests, the tactic incorporated the use of attacks one day and then apologies the next. The attacks were carried out by Bush's handlers, and then Bush would call for an apology on the part of his staffer who made the attack. This was a strategy that was implemented during the convention and continued through the general election. Clearly, the purpose was to plant the seeds of fear about Clinton in the minds of voters and thus maneuver a more negative position for Clinton.[28]

But Clinton kept closer tabs on the needs of the nation and offered voters what they wanted. He was able to accomplish this by responding to all of the accusations made against his character during the primaries, shaping the right image during the convention, and reinforcing his position in the general election with a specific plan to remedy domestic economic woes.[29]

One very effective imagery-building device for Clinton during this stage in the campaign was his constant presence with Gore. Bush's almost constant avoidance of public contact with Dan Quayle reinforced an implicit message that with the election of Clinton voters would get a working vice president but with Bush voters would not.[30] Another effective device used by the Clinton camp during this period was to position Clinton as a so-called new Democrat, who could lead the country through change, as opposed to Bush, who was portrayed as a president who was living in the past.[31]

During this period in the campaign, the debates corroborated both Bush's and Clinton's standing in the polls and propelled Perot to higher standing because of his excellent performance. Throughout the first two debates, Clinton held a sizable lead in the polls based in part on his grasp of the details of a broad range of issues. Clinton was able to articulate his points well and after the first debate looked as presidential as Bush did. But in the second debate Clinton made his best impression partly because the format uniquely incorporated voters' direct questions. Because this format was used by Clinton throughout the primary season, he was very comfortable with it. Clinton thus supported his image as a strong leader and showed in the second debate that he was in touch with people's feelings.[32]

Perot won the first debate, according to most analysts who watched it. He was witty, clever, and always forced Bush and Clinton to stick to the issues. Bush finally found his center in the third debate but was unable to make up for lost time. Bush's performance in especially the first two debates reinforced the image of a president too distant from the concerns of the American people. Perhaps the classic image many voters will remember is Bush looking at his watch during one of the debates, indicating to the viewers that this was not someplace he wanted to be. That small gesture sent a strong message of Bush's discomfort and disengagement.[33]

Perot left the race on July 16 and reentered 76 days later. After he left the race, some media analysts believed that he immediately began strategizing about his reentry, which eventually materialized. In the process of this vacillation, he successfully disoriented the press enough to remove himself from the spotlight, which may have been the real reason for leaving the race.[34]

During this period, Perot was able to convince voters that he was serious about change and effectively set up a position for himself based on some radical proposals, including changes in health care, instituting a gasoline tax, and others. The perception that he was too thin-skinned and not patient enough to be a leader of this country contributed to the decreased momentum of support. But by the end of the campaign Perot was still able to attract a loyal following of voters who were convinced that he was the man to lead the nation. This was not only a major accomplishment for an independent candidate but will set the foundation for Perot's presence in American politics for years to come.

Conclusion

Positioning candidates, as opposed to products, is a complicated task because voters' decisions change much more quickly than consumers' do. Take, for example, the case of Perot, who went from the top of the polls in the summer and then down to the bottom after he pulled out of the race. How could voter choices change so radically? Is it possible to map just as quickly the change in voters' minds? Voters' minds change quickly because of the intensity of media coverage of the candidates during the primaries. Consequently, when candidates either win or lose crucial primaries, their standing in the polls changes and in tandem the decisions of the voters. However, sophisticated computer technology enables the candidates' organizations to quickly map voter decision changes.

Clinton's success can be attributed to the flexibility he maintained throughout the campaign, beginning with a message of change that resonated well in the ears of voters throughout the primary season. However, once he entered the convention stage, Clinton repositioned his theme of change around the economy. Bush, on the other hand, was trying to reposition his image from the time he won the war in Iraq. He seemed to be fixed on the image of himself as a leader of the Western world and the one candidate who could be relied on in the case of a crisis.

In the end, the image of Clinton as a leader who would bring about change in the economy won him the election. Bush's downfall was due to the disparity between the image he had created in his own mind and the one that translated into the minds of voters. Perot's offer to be the servant of the people was clearly an attractive position but not potent enough to win the election for him.

The next chapter turns to the last part of the marketing campaign: strategy formulation and implementation.

Notes

1. Clinton/Gore campaign (1992).
2. Clinton/Gore campaign (1992).
3. Clinton/Gore campaign (1992).
4. Nimmo (1974), pp. 771-781.
5. For a good discussion of the methodological issues related to the development of the positioning map, see Johnson (1971), pp. 13-18.
6. *Time* (1992, September 14), p. 36.

7. *USA Today* (1992, November 4).
8. *Time* (1991, December 30), p. 19.
9. *Time* (1992, January 27), p. 22.
10. *Time* (1992, January 27), p. 22.
11. *U.S. News and World Report* (1992, February 10), p. 24.
12. *The New York Times* (1992, February 25).
13. *The New York Times* (1992, March 20).
14. *The New York Times* (1992, February 25).
15. *The New York Times* (1992, August 3).
16. *The New York Times* (1992, July 17).
17. *The New York Times* (1992, July 10).
18. *The New York Times* (1992, July 13).
19. *The New York Times* (1992, July 17).
20. *The New York Times* (1992, July 17).
21. *The New York Times* (1992, July 21).
22. *The New York Times* (1992, August 10).
23. *The New York Times* (1992, August 10).
24. *The New York Times* (1992, August 24).
25. *The New York Times* (1992, June 3).
26. *U.S. News and World Report* (1992, September 23), p. 34.
27. *U.S. News and World Report* (1992, September 14), p. 32.
28. *The New York Times* (1992, August 20).
29. *The New York Times* (1992, September 28).
30. *The New York Times* (1992, September 8).
31. *The New York Times* (1992, September 28).
32. *The New York Times* (1992, October 21).
33. *The New York Times* (1992, October 21).
34. *Newsweek* (1992, October 12), p. 30.

★ 6 ★

Strategy Formulation and Implementation

As the candidate moves through the stages of the campaign, he must put together a cohesive strategy that can be used to reinforce his chosen position. In this chapter, I discuss the strategic plan, the blueprint behind the formulation, and implementation of a strategy (see Figure 6.1). At the heart of the strategic plan are the "four Ps," a strategy commonly followed in the commercial marketplace.[1] For a company marketing a product, the four Ps include the following components: product, promotion, price, and place (also referred to as distribution). The strategy a candidate follows closely mirrors these four components.

In the candidate's strategy the first P is the *product*, which for a candidate is defined in terms of his leadership and campaign platform, particularly issues and policies advocated by him. The next P is called *push marketing*, which refers to the grass-roots effort necessary to build up a volunteer network

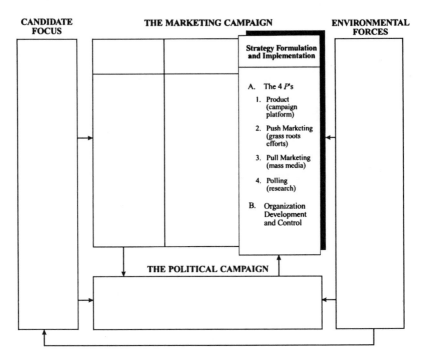

Figure 6.1. Strategy Formulation and Implementation in the Model of Political Marketing

to handle the day-to-day activities in running the campaign. This component is similar to place or the distribution channel that is used to get the product from the manufacturer to the consumer. In politics, the distribution channel centers on transferring information as opposed to a product. The grass-roots effort that is established becomes one information channel that transmits the candidate's message from his organization to the voter.

The third *P* refers to *pull marketing*, which is similar to promotion. Pull marketing becomes a second information channel for the candidate. Instead of the person-to-person channel used with a push marketing approach, this channel makes use of mass media outlets such as television, radio, newspapers, magazines, direct mail, videocassette, and any other form of promotion that is available. It is referred to as pull marketing because the goal is to promote directly to the voter and in a sense pull him or her into the voting booth on election day in a way comparable to the way a consumer would be pulled into a retail outlet after seeing a product advertised on television.

Finally, the fourth *P* in the political marketplace is *polling*, which represents the data analysis and research that are used to develop and test new ideas and determine how successful the ideas will be. This is part of the candidate's marketing strategy because of the consumer orientation candidates use in politics today. Candidates need polls and marketing research to both formulate and implement strategy. Polling replaces price as the fourth *P* because there is not a direct connection between price and politics, although the point could be stretched and an argument made that there is a price that comes with voting for one candidate over another.

The Marketing Strategies of Bush, Clinton, and Perot

The four *P*s are commonly referred to as a marketing strategy and incorporate the tools that will be necessary to reach out to the voter segments targeted by the candidate and solidify his message and image in the minds of voters (see Figure 6.2).

Product (The Campaign Platform)

The development of each of the three candidates' platforms in 1992 varied considerably due to several factors. First, each was working to reinforce a different candidate position. Second, in the case of George Bush and Bill Clinton, their respective political parties had an influence on the establishment of their platforms at their respective national conventions. Third, the personalities and backgrounds of the candidates varied considerably, as did those of the consultants working with them. Finally, although there was some overlap at the time of the general election, each of the candidates had different constituencies, or market segments, to appeal to.

Bush defined his presidency more in terms of maxims than his actual accomplishments. His "Thousand Points of Light" and "kinder and gentler" approach to politics made a deeper imprint on voters' minds than did specific programs. Other than his "no new taxes" pledge, it was difficult to define Bush's platform in 1988, and the same could be said for the one he advocated in 1992. His hope was to build a platform in 1992 on the basis of his own good

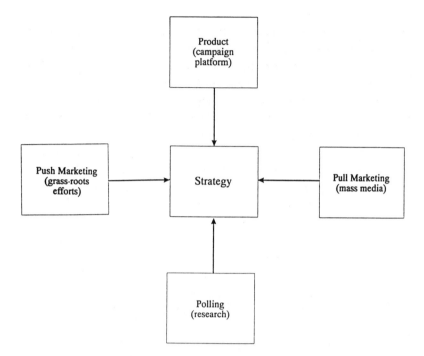

Figure 6.2. Marketing Strategy: The Four *P*s
NOTE: The four *P*s represent the marketing strategy that is used to reinforce the candidate's position in the market.

intentions and his ability to deal with America's problems rather than on any specific programs.[2]

Bush's theme was "leadership based on experience." He asked voters who they thought had the best vision and agenda for the future of the country and who they could trust when unexpected circumstances threatened. This was a reference to the likelihood of the United States participating in another war and the perception that he was a more stable force to deal with it. The three important initiatives that he set out for his first year in office included a program to provide job training and help small businesses, trade initiatives through his North American Free Trade Agreement, and a health care plan that would control costs while making health insurance available to all. Bush accused "Clintonomics" as a move backward to high taxes and regulation. Perhaps Bush's most central theme was character and the fact that Americans need a president they can trust, thus asserting that Clinton could not be trusted.

Bush tried to add some substance to his re-election bid in his State of the Union message but only offered blame for his misjudgment of the economic situation in the country. Although he proposed a tax-cutting program, the plan came too late and was not substantial enough to satisfy most voters. To avoid sending different signals, Bush decided to cut back on his foreign travel, avoid commenting on foreign policy, and instead keep his statements focused on domestic policy.[3]

In general, Bush's platform was centered on family values, with an extension of that theme going beyond families to the country. This never worked for the Republicans and Bush because, in large part, the structure of the family has changed in this country, and the theme became confusing and insulting to some voters. Barbara Bush became the centerpiece of this platform, along with her 5 children and 12 grandchildren, and the Clintons simply could not compete. The Bushes' extended family presented a very attractive portrait to the American people.[4]

Ross Perot's theme was "getting the country moving again" by asking the American people to decide whether they should get on with the business of paying bills and creating jobs or just hope that the problem will go away. Throughout the campaign, Perot emphasized the importance of reducing the national debt, which stood at $4.1 trillion at election time. Perot said he had spelled out a specific solution that would fix the deficit. He asked whether parents wanted their children and grandchildren to keep the American dream alive. And he promised that a vote for him would end the gridlock in Washington and change the way business was done there.

Perot was truly the first candidate ever telemarketed. Implementing all of the techniques discussed in earlier chapters, Perot campaigned in a high-tech way, choosing to transmit his message over the airwaves instead of making campaign appearances, although he made a few token appearances at the end of the campaign. Perot sidestepped the usual campaign process, not participating in the primaries but instead jumping into the fray at debate time. He proposed radical changes in the way the United States is governed, but the greatest influence of his platform was to focus the media's attention toward the issues and away from the images of the candidates.

Clinton's theme was "choosing fundamental change." He suggested that together he and the voters could make this election a victory not just for people or a party but for the American spirit. The choice he framed for the American people was between more of the same versus fundamental change. He accused Bush of asking the American electorate to settle for less. Essentially,

Clinton's program revolved around moving the economic policies away from the Reagan inheritance of trickle-down economics. Clinton proposed to put America back to work by creating a plan that would create 8 million jobs by building roads and highways, retooling factories, retraining workers, and restoring the United States' competitive edge.

According to Paul Begala, a senior Clinton strategist, Clinton's theme was successful because he was able to present a positive message to the American people. Instead of focusing alone on what was wrong with Bush, Clinton had a clear focus on the message he wanted to impart to the American people: Clinton's vision was consistently articulated from the beginning to the end of the campaign. Begala also referred to the strategic focus that Clinton gave the organization with respect to his theme in the campaign. Clinton worked for 12 years to move the Democratic party to a point where he and Al Gore at the end of the Democratic convention were able to say that they were a "different kind of Democrat." This was a metaphor that Clinton then used to promote his message at the end of the campaign, noting that he would be a "different kind of President" as well.[5]

Push Marketing (Grass-Roots Efforts)

One critical information channel for the candidate is the volunteer network (or grass-roots effort) he builds up around the country. The local party and campaign officials in towns operate mini–campaign organizations that solicit help and money from volunteers to support the campaign effort. There are telephone banks that need to be operated; thousands of calls are made to supporters to ensure they will get out and vote on election day. Mailings need to go out on a regular basis, and rallies have to be organized at every campaign stop the candidate makes. All of these activities revolve around the efforts of thousands of campaign workers, most of whom volunteer their time to the candidate's cause. Grass-roots efforts are organized by the consultants, who form a nucleus around the candidate. Within that nucleus are the fund-raising and direct mail experts, who are relied on to finance all of these activities.

Fund-raising is one area that is unique to politics and has its own set of dynamics and issues, many of which have been raised in previous chapters. More important than any other single issue, however, is that fund-raising is the lifeblood of the grass-roots efforts in a campaign organization. Fund-raising in 1992 was not easy, mainly due to the recession. The political action committees representing industries that were suffering financially simply did not have the same amount of money that they had in 1988 to pass on to the political parties. Because of this, candidates relied more heavily on the free exposure they received in the media.[6]

One of the major contributors to the Clinton campaign was Jeremy Jacobs, owner of the country's largest dog racing track, located in Arkansas. Through a technique known in fund-raising circles as "bundling," Jacobs was able to circumvent the federal law that limits contributions of $1,000 per candidate by having family members give $1,000 each, thus raising the effective contribution to $10,000. Clinton was not the only candidate with such contributors, but the example highlights one of the loopholes in the election laws that needs to be changed.[7]

Money is often raised by holding fund-raising events at critical junctures in the campaign. For example, immediately following Clinton's acceptance speech at the democratic convention, Clinton held a fund-raiser at which the least expensive seat cost $1,000 and a total of more than $3 million was raised.[8]

Wall Street firms and the oil and gas industries were the largest contributors to the 1992 presidential candidates. Behind them in magnitude of donations were the insurance, tobacco, and real estate industries. The single largest contributor was the Archer-Daniels-Midland Company from Decatur, Illinois, which was fined $8,000 by the FEC after the election for violating election laws on contributing to individual candidates. Because of the federal limitations on contributions to individual candidates, more contributions now come in to the political party.[9]

The Perot organization was very successful in building an old-fashioned grass-roots organization, even though it was organized in a high-tech manner. However, the transition in Perot's campaign from an organization built mainly on the efforts of volunteers to one that would eventually rely on consultants and computers was not easy for Perot to make. A fear developed among the people who led the petition drive to get Perot's name on the ballot in all 50 states that the consultants who were hired by Perot would take over the organization. In fact, at one point in the campaign, Perot handed over the reins of control to the professionals he had hired.[10]

Perhaps the most important part of building up a grass-roots effort is the personal appearances made by the candidate. The personal appearances help to energize the campaign organization and bring the candidate into face-to-face contact with the people. Few election observers will forget Clinton's marathon tour that ended the campaign, when he campaigned nonstop for 29 hours straight around the country. The question is, why this level of effort when by most accounts the candidate had the election wrapped up? The answer remains in the same strategic thinking that won the campaign for Clinton. Even at the end of the campaign, the Clinton organization wanted to show the American people how energetic and young Clinton was compared to Bush.[11]

Pull Marketing (The Mass Media)

Pull marketing is perhaps the closest link between candidate and product marketing, where the media is used as the vehicle to convey the image and message of the candidate. Local television was used by all three candidates to circumvent the more traditional media outlets and reach voters more directly. It was chosen in part because voter viewership of network news was declining and because of Clinton's inability to reach out with his message through traditional media outlets during the early primaries. He found instead a successful formula with the live call-in shows and adhered to the use of alternate media outlets throughout the rest of the campaign.

In fact, a whole new political reality was created in the 1992 campaign. The television call-in shows became a common scene for all of the candidates. In one live interview with Bush on *CBS This Morning*, questions were directed toward Bush from a live audience for over an hour. The broadcast came live from the Rose Garden at the White House and was one of the few times that Bush used this format. In a political season in which Clinton and Perot had mastered the live media format, Bush was at a disadvantage because of his resistance to it.[12]

Bush handed over his media campaign to Martin Puris and Clayton Wilhite, both presidents of their respective Madison Avenue advertising agencies in charge of some well-known brand-name products, such as Budweiser beer, BMW automobiles, Milk of Magnesia, and others. Neither one had very much experience with political advertising, but the choice of the two outsiders was in reaction to the poor results from the advertising used in New Hampshire by the original people chosen for the job, Don Sipple, Michael Murphy, and Alex Castellanos. Under the direction of Puris and Wilhite, these three advertising executives, along with others, worked in creative teams to bring out a side of Bush that did not come out successfully in New Hampshire. Their goal was to bring out the personal side of Bush in settings that demonstrated him articulating his goals to voters.[13]

The Bush advertising strategy made use of several different avenues to convey an attractive image of Bush to voters. One commercial that played during the summer Olympics showed pictures of ordinary Americans and Russians talking about Bush's leadership. This type of advertisement, in which voters were seen talking about his accomplishments and the vast experience he brought to his presidency, highlighted Bush's credentials.[14] In a similar vein, Bush's media consultants refocused the theme of change to imply that it must be directed by principle for it to be successful. This image was conveyed by a commercial that started out by zeroing in on the presidential seal and then fading into a close-up of Bush's face, at which point he started to speak in a very sincere manner.[15]

The Bush camp played on the theme of change, but they realized, albeit too late, that change was the dominant hot button in the minds of voters. However, their general approach was to tie change in with the bodies of government not including the president, namely, the need to change Congress or the cabinet. Bush advertising attempted to suggest to the American voters that they could reject the status quo and at the same time vote for Bush, although this strategy did not work out.[16]

In strategic terms, Bush moved into attack mode against his opponents after the New Hampshire primary results indicated that Pat Buchanan was a real threat. But Bush had no problem with negative ads because of the distinction he made between campaigning and running the country. When it came to campaigning, in a word, almost anything went according to Bush. Bush often separated campaigning from governing and was quick to point out that although he was very careful on how he governed he saw campaigning more as open warfare and felt more freedom to do whatever it took to win, within reason.[17]

There were a whole host of negative commercials aired against Clinton as well. In one commercial, there were close-ups of voters in a park talking about Clinton, saying that Clinton has not been telling the truth and that to be president one needs to be honest.[18] In another commercial, Clinton's tax proposal was attacked: The voiceover described what the taxes would mean to the average taxpayer and suggested that taxes would in fact increase, not decrease.[19] The most negative advertisements were aired on the radio, via which Bush first brought up the draft issue against Clinton. In one radio commercial, an announcer took the listener through a chronological series of events that tied into the draft issue, then talked about how Clinton at first said he never received a draft notice but later reversed his story. The announcer went on to relate that Clinton said he respected the military but then never joined.[20] In these cases, Bush was trying to reinforce the image of Clinton as a "waffler."

But, as the campaign edged toward election day, Bush held fewer and fewer press conferences and became more cautious in his effort to avoid making any glaring mistakes. The image of Bush as a world leader, however, continued to come out in the press. Curiously, Quayle was very quiet during most of the campaign, especially when it came to the commercials, in which he was rarely seen. His campaign schedule placed him in environments that limited the chances of attacks against him. Only after the convention did Quayle begin to draw larger and more enthusiastic crowds.[21]

Clinton's advertising strategy was similar to the Republican strategy of hiring Madison Avenue executives, but for Clinton they created only positive commercials. Political advertising experts were hired to develop the negative spots. The Clinton camp hired Donny Deutsch, creative director of his own firm and responsible for the innovative advertisements for the Ikea line of home furnishings. Although there was some criticism of the work that Frank Greer had done in heading up the advertising for the primaries, his partner, Mandy Grunwald, led the advertising effort after the convention. With Grunwald directing several of the creative teams of Madison Avenue executives, the Clinton approach closely resembled the tactics used by Bush.[22] In particular, Clinton wanted to avoid the mistakes made in the Dukakis campaign, the media team of which was so disorganized that commercials lacked a unified theme.

In a very innovative turn at the Democratic convention, party officials developed the Convention Satellite News Service. This service provided free prepackaged soundbites to local stations not able to afford to send a reporter to the convention. The very organized and cohesive group running the Democratic convention also carefully scrutinized every speech given to ensure that the theme of putting people first came across loud and clear.

Likewise, Clinton's team distributed a one-page bulletin every day that gave convention-goers pointers on what to say when interviewed on television. For example, in one bulletin handed out at the convention, Clinton was quoted as saying that Jesse Jackson's speech the night before was powerful and that both Clinton and Jackson were advocating the same economic agenda. When Dennis Hayden, executive producer at the convention and formerly with the MacNeil/Lehrer program, was asked if he was in effect packaging Clinton, he replied that the purpose of the convention was to disseminate information to the voters in a manner similar to that in a news operation.[23]

Clinton's strategy at the convention was to respond to the accusations thrown at him during the primaries by presenting a biography of Clinton that would reinforce his positive qualities as a human being and at the same time allow him to advance his policies to the American people.[24] Throughout his media appearances from the convention on, Clinton's goal was to direct voters' attention to the issues that mattered the most to them, especially the economy.

Although Clinton also used negative advertising, the attacks were centered more on Bush's policies and record as president than on his character. In addition, Clinton attacked the press. In one ad, an announcer talked about how Clinton stood up to the press's false attacks on him; the ad then went into Clinton's background and how he spent his life committed to fighting for what he believes in. His years as a Rhodes Scholar, his education at Georgetown and Yale, and his record as governor of Arkansas were high-lighted, and the ad ended by affirming how Clinton would help the middle class by putting people first.[25]

In one of his negative spots against Bush, Clinton explained how Bush put into law the second biggest tax hike in the history of this country. He then compared this policy blemish to his record as governor of Arkansas, noting how his state had the second lowest tax rate per person in the country. This commercial was couched in a catch phrase, "getting the facts straight."[26] Another negative spot filled the screen with an image of Bush, slightly out of focus, talking about how robust the economy was. As he was speaking, a voiceover posed a question: If Bush doesn't understand the problem, then how will he be able to solve it?[27]

In ads with a more positive slant, the Clinton/Gore bus tour moved around the country and stopped for visits with ordinary-looking people along the side of the road who waved flags and smiled, and Clinton reached out to shake their hands. The next shots showed Clinton working behind his desk in the governor's mansion and then delivering his address at the convention. Words flashed across the last image, stating that Clinton would be a president who cares about people and who would work for them.[28] In another commercial, Clinton talked about getting people off of welfare using his plan to educate Americans and get them working again. At the end of the commercial, an

"800" number was flashed on the screen for anyone interested in seeing a copy of his plan.[29]

Clinton also relied on radio commercials to communicate his most negative messages. In one, the president is accused of ducking the debates. After an announcer goes through a long list of economic statistics, he points out that Americans must have many questions and that voters should have a chance to hear the candidates debate. The commercial ends by asking why Bush will not debate Clinton. In addition to acting as an avenue for candidates to communicate negative messages about their opponents, radio commercials allowed the candidates to more effectively target specific audiences.[30]

While Bush and Clinton continued their battle over the airwaves, Perot introduced the American people to a new form of political communication, namely, the infomercial. Instead of using 30- and 60-second commercials, Perot used several half-hour programs to relay his view that the economy was in terrible shape and that something had to be done about it.[31] Perot financed his campaign with his own money, which at least partly explains why he used the more cost-effective television infomercials as often as he did.

Many skeptics thought that it was impossible to keep the attention of the American voter for a half-hour of information conveyed through the use of diagrams and charts, but they were wrong. Perot's commercials were in some cases more popular than the situation comedy programs on the air at the same time. This was due in part to his novel use of media aids, such as a "voodoo stick" to reinforce the idea that Bush's programs were based on magic, not sound thinking. The A. C. Nielson company estimated that one 30-minute commercial, aired on a Friday night, was watched by around 13 million people.

But Clinton's likewise unorthodox use of advertising dollars paid off for him, according to Grunwald, his media chief. The Clinton camp spent less money on network television than any other presidential campaign in history, and, according to Grunwald, it was a gamble. One begins to get a sense of the strategic unity in this organization when looking closely at its advertising strategy. The media organizers did not advertise on television at all in their top-end states (i.e., those they were sure they would win). Their assumption was that a 30-point lead, which they held in most of these states, would at most drift down to a 15- or 20-point lead, thus saving them millions of dollars in resources to spend elsewhere. The gamble was to leave their top-end states unprotected, but, as history shows, the gamble paid off.[32]

All of their advertising dollars were spent in the battleground states (i.e., those that were undecided). In the words of Grunwald, they ran a Senate-level campaign in these states, which meant going on the air before Labor Day, another very unorthodox strategy. In effect, their advertising dollars went into only the 32 states they targeted. In Michigan, for example, where Clinton was up in the polls by only about 4 to 6 percentage points before Labor Day, this strategy enabled him to build his lead to double-digits by late September. Bush was just beginning to go on the air in late September, when it was too late for him to break such a sizable lead. In addition, Bush centered his advertising on network television, which, because of its high costs for advertising, limited his coverage in those states. In every one of the battleground states, Clinton had television spots that aired more frequently than Bush's commercials.[33]

From a message point of view, senior Clinton strategist Begala pointed out two tracks of promotion used in the campaign. One track centered on Bush's failure to keep his promises and and on his job performance. A second track adhered to Clinton's economic plan and vision for the new direction he wanted for the country. This plan was supported by his record in Arkansas and his desire to work hard for the American people. All along, the people in the Clinton camp wanted to remind voters why they were turning away from Bush and, at the same time, why they could be so hopeful with a Clinton/Gore ticket.[34]

There was always an effort in the Clinton camp to keep the race close to the two tracks identified, especially on Bush's economic performance in office. A big part of Clinton's success was his ability to stay focused on these two tracks throughout the campaign. This was accomplished by using what Grunwald called very straightforward and effective spots that focused on Clinton's own words and record in office.

These spots emphasized Clinton's record as a different kind of Democrat, with several of the advertisements referring to his record in Arkansas on issues including welfare reform, the death penalty, and a balanced budget. These messages sent a clear signal that Clinton was not a traditional liberal, contrary to the image that the Bush camp was trying to paint of him in their advertising.[35]

Polling (Research)

The last of the four *P*s is polling, which includes any form of information that is used to help develop the candidate's campaign strategy and communicate it to the various publics. This is introduced as one of the four *P*s because of the important roles that research and polling play in marketing a candidate. The time pressures and tremendous degree of flexibility that is necessary to run a successful campaign demonstrate the need for an effective information feedback system that will allow the candidate to alter his marketing strategy on the spot.

Several innovations were used in the course of the 1992 campaign, including "900" and "800" telephone numbers, creative applications of focus groups, moment-to-moment research (a sophisticated technology that tracks voter responses to commercials second by second), and others. The pollster has become one of the key power brokers in the electoral process. The dependence on the insight and professional expertise of the pollster determines how a campaign strategy will shift during the course of the political campaign. In many ways, polling has become to political marketing what research and development is to a corporation; both are responsible for innovation of the product.

The polls were watched very closely by all three candidates, especially at the end of the race. Stan Greenberg, Clinton's pollster, discounted any hint of a closing between Clinton and Bush, and the final percentages in the popular vote closely matched Greenberg's numbers in the final week of the campaign. In fact, Greenberg suggested that there was a settling of a 7-point margin during the last week of the campaign. This closely matched the final percentages in the popular vote, of which Clinton had 43%, Bush 38%, and Perot 19%.[36]

The information generated during the course of the campaign sets the foundation for the candidate to segment his market of voters and to position himself. In addition to the candidates, however, the pollsters, political parties, political action committees, and the media also rely on this information technology to pursue their goals. Two of the most commonly used tools in 1992 were focus groups and polls.

Focus Groups

Although focus groups have been used in marketing for decades to test out new product concepts, to get consumer reactions to advertising appeals, and for several other purposes, they have become extremely popular in politics. The following technical definition of *focus groups* highlights the key aspects of this political research tool:

Focus groups are a small number of individuals with known demographic characteristics brought together for an informal and open discussion of issues framed
by a pollster and often raised by a moderator. For the candidate, the strategic
implication is to define the candidate for the electorate. This technique is used
as a complement to sample surveys of public opinion. By virtue of the free-
flowing conversation that is encouraged, focus groups make it possible to
explore the terms of reference within which people view an issue, how they react
to the views of others, and how people work through an issue that is new to
them or with which they may be uncomfortable.[37]

Individuals are chosen for focus groups based on certain criteria or patterns
of response to earlier polls. One of the problems with focus groups is that
they are by definition unrepresentative of a targeted population. However,
focus groups can be used to complement public opinion research by acquainting
pollsters with other dimensions of the voters' thinking. In turn, questions are
worded for polls and questionnaires based on focus group results.[38]

Polls

One of the most influential tools used in modern-day political campaigns
is the poll. It represents a snapshot of the thinking of the electorate. One
distinction that should be made at the outset is the subtle but important
difference between polling and marketing research. Polling presents a de-
scriptive overview of various segments of the electorate at different points
in time. Through the use of sophisticated statistical analysis, marketing
research is used to isolate and explain dimensions of the candidate's strategy
that cannot be determined by polling alone.

Polls are most often used to give an overall description as opposed to a
deep analysis of why voters think the way they do. The reason for this is that
polls are usually used for media consumption and therefore must be concise
and easy to interpret. They also track the horse race mentality of a campaign
by predicting who is ahead of whom. Sampling is key to polling to ensure
that the results can be generalized to the entire electorate.

There are several varieties of polls and surveys, including the following:

- benchmark surveys—usually conducted after a candidate has decided to seek
  office; designed to provide a baseline from which to evaluate the subsequent
  campaign; collects standard information about the public image of candidates,
  their positions on issues, and the demographics of the electorate;

- trial heat surveys—not a survey but a question or series of questions within a survey, such as grouping candidates together in hypothetical match-ups and asking citizens who they would vote for in the hypothetical pairing;
- tracking polls—conducted by a campaign, most often on a daily basis near election day to monitor closely any late shifts in support, provide up-to-date information on which to base any last-minute shifts in campaign strategy and media advertising;
- cross-sectional and panel surveys—multiple polls conducted by major polling organizations over time on an election contest, use different samples of citizens for each round of interviews, provide a picture of where the electorate stood at a single point in time; and
- exit polls— carried out immediately after the voter casts his or her ballot.[39]

Exit polls have become very popular with the media, especially in their reporting of election results, in order to get an immediate read on the public. Exit polls sample voters only and interview them on election day, thus eliminating many of the costs of carrying out a random sample. The sampling is critical in conducting this type of research. The process usually begins with a complete list of all precincts in the jurisdiction (usually a state) for which the exit poll is being conducted. Then a sample of precincts is drawn and the questionnaire, usually containing about three dozen questions printed on both sides of a mock ballot, is distributed.

Call-in polls (with 900 and 800 phone numbers) are also used relatively frequently by the media and by some pollsters interested in reading response immediately after a debate. AT&T, for example, provides the mechanism for the poll and markets the service to the broadcast media. Unfortunately, this sort of poll is terribly unreliable from a sampling perspective. The 900-number polls, used almost exclusively by the media, could be very misleading because the people who call in may not be representative of the general population.

In recent years, the mass media's work with poll data has increased, resulting in the institutionalization of in-house polling operations by newspapers, magazines, and television networks. The news media have begun to report on elections using polls as a major source of information. In fact, the polls have become the focus of modern-day campaigns because they play a major role in setting the media's campaign agenda.

The debate about the relative merit of polls is widespread. One area of concern is the impact of polls on the bandwagon effect. According to one assessment,

Some scholars contend that the continual release of poll results throughout the campaign creates a "bandwagon effect." As poll results and media reports begin to show a solid trend, the public's opinion solidifies in the direction of that trend. Polling reports are believed to cause public opinion and to create momentum in favor of the leading candidate. The bandwagon effect is attributed to the ease with which the press is able to transmit information about winning and losing as well as to the reasonably accurate perception of the public concerning the impact of that information.[40]

The effects of polls on businesses and consumers is explained well by Bradburn and Sudman:

If one believes that legitimate businesses can continue to exist and to be profitable only if they satisfy consumer needs, then the role of the polls is obvious. A firm cannot satisfy consumer needs if it does not know what those needs are. Thus, surveys are used to provide information that enables a business to serve the consumer better. . . . If one believes, however, that businesses manipulate consumers into purchasing unneeded or harmful items, then the polls must also be held responsible as one of the tools of the devil. . . . Marketing based on polls can be used to get people to try a new product, but only satisfaction with product performance can make people continue to use it. Most firms depend on customer satisfaction for their own continuing prosperity, and many place heavy emphasis on surveys of their own customers to uncover and thus be able to correct quickly any causes of dissatisfaction.[41]

Another dimension of research that is relied on extensively to develop the candidate's marketing strategy is opposition research. Although there is nothing new about digging to find out any tidbit of information about your opponent that might be used against him during the course of the campaign, what is new is the level of sophistication to which this process has evolved. There were two people responsible for this type of research in each political party in 1992: Dan Carol for the Democrats and David Tell for the Republicans. Both in their 30s, they had the responsibility for combing through information to find anything of interest about the opposition, including past voting records, tax statements, and so on. Carol and Tell operated out of ordinary offices, using the most sophisticated computers available at the time, which were the Lexis and Nexis systems. These systems allowed them to retrieve press clippings and a whole host of other documents by simply pressing a button.[42]

The Strategic Plan

The campaign organization's strategic plan is the blueprint for winning the election. The strategic plan brings together the same elements that one finds in a business organization; in fact, running a political organization is very similar to running a business organization because both operate on the same rudimentary principles. A strategic plan hinges on the development of a solid organization that sets goals and strategies for the candidate at each stage in the campaign. The goals and strategies interactively develop before they are finalized. Once the organization's people are in place and the final goals have been established, three systems must be installed to effectively carry out the marketing strategy: a strategy formulation system, a strategy implementation system, and a system to monitor and control the activities of the organization. Figure 6.3 depicts each of the steps in the strategic plan.

Organizational Development (The Consultants)

Organizing the campaign team includes the designation of responsibilities and the chain of command. This process closely resembles organizational structuring in a business operation, although the duties and responsibilities vary. Unlike the business world, the task in a political organization often centers on the ability of the candidate to harness a volunteer network. Many volunteer workers hope to land a job in the government, the possibilities of which are greater assuming that the candidate wins office.

Without the most talented consultants and professionals it is virtually impossible to put together an organization that can effectively operate. There is tremendous competition to get the best professionals possible, and that is often a function of both the philosophy espoused by the candidate and the perception that the candidate can win in November. Any consultant knows that working for a winning presidential candidate is a ticket to success in his or her consulting business.

In addition to the hiring of consultants, the choice of a running mate deserves special attention. According to the more traditional approach to this decision, a Southern presidential candidate would look to round out his ticket and thus not choose another Southerner. But, then again, politics does not operate in the same way that it used to in this country. As an agent of change, Clinton chose Gore for his running mate to send a signal that he would not be following the path of least resistance in his bid for the White House but

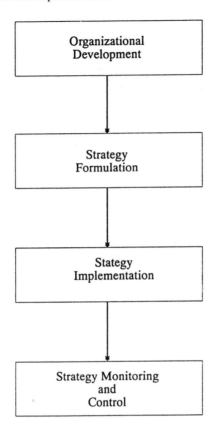

Figure 6.3. The Strategic Plan
NOTE: The strategic plan is the overall blueprint that delineates the activities of the campaign organization.

instead would be daring. His choice of Gore was certainly a good one, as we all know now because the Clinton/Gore ticket won. Gore not only campaigned well but made no mistakes and added credibility to Clinton because of his excellent record in Congress and clean history.[43]

Perot's choice of James Stockdale for running mate was one of the lessons of 1992 in the enormous importance of this choice. Stockdale's performance was not up to par with Gore's and Quayle's performance, as most keenly felt in the debates. As it will be shown, Perot also had difficulty attracting political consultants.

Any good organization must delineate the tasks of all of its members. A good example of the importance of creating the appropriate task chart can be seen in the failure of the Bush organization. When Baker came on board, he became the decision maker on almost every major activity, including scheduling and speeches. But perhaps even more important in defining the roles of people in the campaign organization is the impact they have on the candidate's emotional makeup. This is where some say Baker made the most influence. Bush changed after Baker joined the campaign: His speeches came across more effectively and the messages sent out were more consistent. Inconsistency was in large part Bush's problem up until the convention. His messages often changed from day to day and speech to speech. Baker tried to give Bush's communications to voters direction and a vision, which is the ultimate task of any campaign organization.[44]

But Bush never got off on the right foot in this campaign. His organization was developed late in the campaign and seemed to be disorganized throughout. His campaign was cochaired by Robert Teeter, a pollster by training, and Samuel Skinner, who rose to become the chief of staff after John Sununu left the administration. Eventually, the organization was rebuilt when James Baker took over in August. Baker brought with him a team that made quick decisions and eliminated meetings that failed to accomplish the tasks at hand prior to his coming on board. In addition, a problem with leaks of information was mysteriously brought to a halt.[45]

Baker had successfully masterminded Bush's 1988 campaign, and many political analysts in the media thought he could do the same in 1992. Although Baker found an unorganized group running the campaign when he entered it, he was unwilling to fire many of the staffers for fear of creating the illusion (or reflecting the reality) that the campaign was in a tailspin. Baker had a core group of his aides—Margaret Tutwiler, Robert Zoellick, Dennis Ross, and Janet Mullins—take over the day-to-day operation of the campaign. All of these aides came from the State Department with Baker and worked with several Bush officials every day. Each morning the group met with Richard Darman, the budget director, Robert Teeter, Fred Malek, Brent Scowcroft, the National Security adviser, and Marlin Fitzwater, the press secretary.[46] With this team, Baker unsuccessfully tried to repackage the theme of the campaign from change to trust. By asking voters who they trusted, Baker thought he could redirect the focus of the voters and the media. Bush also suggested using Baker as his economic czar for a second term in the hopes of winning over the hearts and minds of the American electorate, but the strategy failed.[47]

All of the candidates relied heavily on consultants to help them shape their campaign platforms and images but none more so than Clinton. His campaign manager at the start of the campaign was Mickey Kantor, a Los Angeles lawyer who knew the Clintons for several years. He became more actively involved in the campaign shortly before the New Hampshire primary, when the tabloids began to publish stories about Clinton's infidelity. Later in the campaign, Kantor became the chief executive of the organization, which allowed David Wilhelm to step in as campaign manager. Wilhelm's responsibility revolved around the coordination of strategy on a regional basis.[48]

Clinton's image builders were Greer and Grunwald, partners in a Democratic firm. James Carville and Begala, also partners in a consulting firm, made the day-to-day strategic decisions, with Carville operating out of Little Rock and Begala going on the road with Clinton. Begala was the chief speechwriter, and Carville was in charge of putting together the one-liners and responses to bad press that came out.[49] The issues director was Bruce Reed, who then became Gore's campaign manager. Dee Dee Myers served as press secretary, Raham Emmanuel as finance director, and Eli Segal was in charge of management, budget, and personnel in the campaign.[50]

Carville became a top Democratic consultant by devising the 1991 upset victory of Harris Wofford, who ran for the Pennsylvania Senate. Carville then joined Clinton's campaign in November 1991. Carville was in charge of the strategies and sound bites for the campaign. His approach to the campaign was to never let a charge against Clinton stand without hitting back immediately. George Stephanopoulos was the deputy communications director for the 1988 Michael Dukakis campaign, and then after the 1988 election, he worked for Richard Gephardt in a staff position. Stephanopoulos became communications director for the Clinton campaign and was responsible for overseeing public relations, polling, speeches, research, and all advertising decisions.[51]

Grunwald and Greer were in charge of putting together the media strategy and successfully placed Clinton and his family on the covers of the nation's leading magazines. Furthermore, Clinton relied on the assistance of his friend and television producer, Linda Bloodworth-Thomason, to develop the biographical film that was shown at the convention. Bloodworth-Thomason and her husband were the coproducers of "Designing Women" and "Evening Shade" and helped Clinton prepare for his many live television appearances. For example, Mr. Thomason telephoned *The Arsenio Hall Show* to set up the television appearance for Clinton.

One of the more important roles the consultants played in the 1992 campaign was in changing the focus of Clinton's news coverage. This feat is credited to Betsey Wright, a Clinton aide from Little Rock who was responsible for fighting back against the reporters who pursued negative information about Clinton's background.[52] Both Clinton and Wright worked on the 1972 George McGovern campaign. Clinton asked Wright to run his campaign for governor after he was defeated for re-election in 1980, and Wright accepted Clinton's offer immediately. After winning back the Governor's mansion, Clinton made Wright his chief of staff, a post she held until 1990. Upon Clinton's entry into the presidential campaign, Wright returned to Little Rock to run the campaign's research operation. She quickly rose to become deputy campaign chairperson as a result of her abilities as an astute archivist.[53]

The so-called war room in Little Rock was a concept developed by Carville, Grunwald, and Stan Greenberg, Clinton's pollster, all of whom decided that the organization needed a single voice to direct strategy. Operated out of Little Rock mainly due to the fact that Clinton's daughter, Chelsea, was living there, the war room's main purpose was to keep Clinton on top of events as they developed each day. In this capacity, aides monitored news events and the latest polls in the media throughout the night, in addition to keeping in touch with the various state headquarters. Scheduling and strategy were discussed at the morning meetings after Carville, Grunwald, and Stephanopoulos arrived, using a report that was waiting for them from the overnight crew. This operation enabled Clinton to stay on track with his voter message and placed him in a position to respond immediately to crises.[54]

The word was out early in the summer of 1992 that political consultants from both parties were being approached by the Perot organization to work for them. This list included John Sears (Ronald Reagan's campaign manager in 1980), Raymond D. Strother (Gary Hart's media consultant in 1984), and Scott Miller (Paul Tsongas's media consultant), among others. None of these consultants took up Perot on his offer, however, for fear they would never get any work in the future.[55]

Perot, who said in the campaign's early stages that he would not allow handlers to run his campaign, eventually succumbed to their influence. Perot hired two of the best consultants: Ed Rollins, a Republican consultant, and Hamilton Jordan, a Democratic consultant. It was certainly a coup in some regard to get these two men to sign up with Perot. But Rollins, who had worked for Ronald Reagan, left only two months after joining Perot over a disagreement on when and how he thought Perot should promote himself.

Rollins believed it was critical that Perot begin advertising immediately to define himself. But Perot disagreed and that frustrated Rollins and several other consultants who were signed up to work with him. Rollins left at a time when the tensions were already running high between the state political coordinators and the hired political consultants, an event that was unavoidable as the Perot candidacy took on more credibility. Jordan, who had worked for Jimmy Carter, also left soon after Rollins.[56]

In addition to Rollins and Jordan, Perot hired two of his business associates to help run his campaign. Morton H. Meyerson worked as an informal adviser in the spring of 1992. He started out as a computer programmer in 1965, became a close associate of Perot, and has been president at E.D.S. corporation since 1979. He succeeded Perot as chair and chief executive of Perot Systems. Perot chose Thomas W. Luce, a legal adviser, to organize a campaign to place Perot's name on the ballot in all 50 states. Luce was then advanced to the head of the petition campaign over Jordan and Rollins.[57]

After his campaign fell apart, Perot brought in Orson Swindle to head up his organization. Previously, Swindle had been his liaison to volunteers in the field. Clayton Mulford, Perot's son-in-law, helped to get him on the ballot in all 50 states, while Sharon Holman, who had worked for Perot since 1969, became his press secretary. Swindle had been a congressional district chair in his native Georgia during Ronald Reagan's 1980 race. Swindle was a personal friend of Perot's for several years and in many ways represented the ideal Perot subordinate: very loyal, efficient, and acquiescent. Murphy Martin was Perot's media chief, a former Dallas TV anchor and longtime Perot associate who was instrumental in producing television and radio ads for the campaign. James Squire, a former editor of the *Chicago Tribune*, became Perot's new press secretary.[58]

There was some disagreement among Perot's consultants regarding who to target and exactly how to publicize his message. Perot hired Joe Canzeri, a Republican advance man, to make sure that the crowds were plentiful at rallies. He also hired Tim Kraft, Carter's field boss in 1976, to organize the field operation around the country. Kraft hired 30 people who were responsible for setting up offices in several states and targeting voters in the congressional districts in those states. John White, Carter's Deputy Budget Director, was put in charge of developing issues and positions. So, in effect, Perot may have started out his campaign as a neophyte politician, but in the end he also relied on consultants and not only volunteers to run his organization.[59]

Strategy Formulation

The first step in formulating a strategy is to conduct a market analysis, which includes a review of several factors. Every potential candidate who thought about running for the presidency in 1992 had to consider the status of the country in light of the rest of the world: How did the United States fare economically, socially, and politically? The answer to this question indicates the general welfare of the country and the likelihood of unseating the incumbent, in this case Bush. The answer to this question did not sit very well with most Democrats because Bush had just accomplished his Iraqi war victory, and he was at his peak in the polls. In addition, each prospective candidate had to look at the issues and concerns of the country at that point in time.

If the candidate is convinced that the time is right to enter the race, then he must take stock of his internal situation and see if it is logical for him to pursue the presidency. One of the most critical decisions at this juncture in the process regards his current obligations and whether or not he has the time and can put forth the effort to devote to this monumental obligation. The candidate looks at his own background and searches into the past for possibly incriminating actions or decisions before someone else does it for him. If the uncovered past reveals controversy, the candidate must figure out whether to take a reactionary stance, respond to charges, or come out and apologize before the campaign even begins.

Finally, there is the necessity for the candidate to look deep within himself to see how motivated he is and whether he has the stamina and courage to jump into the public arena in a way that he has never had to before. Certainly, the Clintons found out that running for the presidency exposed them in a spotlight that was hundreds of degrees hotter than the one they had to go under when Bill was running to become governor of Arkansas.

Next, a serious competitive analysis must be conducted with an eye on the other candidates who have either announced their candidacy or who are considering it in the near future. Early in the process, there was much discussion within the Clinton camp about whether Clinton would run or not if Gore decided to. In addition, there was much trepidation about Mario Cuomo's decision to run because it would seriously affect Clinton's chances if he decided to. At this stage the candidate must make up his mind and determine his purpose for running and his chances of winning. In other words, will the candidacy be a dry heat for the next time around, with the intention of building up name recognition, or will it be to win this time around? This question is sometimes not answered until the candidate reaches the competitive analysis step. In fact, many said that only when Clinton knew for sure that Cuomo was not running did he realize this would not be a dry heat but for real.

Strategy Implementation

The implementation of strategy follows a traditional business orientation with the following variations. First, strategy implementation in a presidential campaign must be extremely flexible because the twists and turns in the course of the election can be very sharp. The level of flexibility must be the greatest during the primaries, when the life of the campaign can rest on the outcome of a single primary election.

Until the primaries, the game is very different. The candidates jockey for position within the party, and their strategy must be implemented in a way that leaves the perception that they are serious contenders. A critical factor for the successful implementation of a candidate's strategy is his identity in the minds of voters. This is something referred to as "brand recognition" in the commercial marketplace, that is, the degree to which the consumer is aware of the name of a company's brand. Likewise, the candidate running for president must become a so-called household word for voters. It is not uncommon for candidates to run for president once or twice just to achieve this goal.

Getting through the primaries requires a tremendous amount of jockeying for the best and brightest consultants. There was a high degree of speculation about each of the Democratic candidates as they came closer to the first primary election. In fact, they were watched closely to see which of the top consultants in the country hopped onto whose bandwagon. Many believed that Clinton was a serious contender when he hired Stephanopoulos and Carville. It was rumored at the time that Stephanopoulos was waiting to see if Gephardt would run before going along with Clinton. When Gephardt decided not to run, Clinton hired one of his first serious consultants.

Once through the primaries and as the candidates move into the convention, the implementation of the strategy takes a serious shift. At the convention, everything depends on whether or not the candidate has consolidated his power base among the delegates and the voters. As the campaign moves into the final leg of the race, from Labor Day on, the implementation of the strategy must be carried out with sharp focus.

Monitoring and Controlling the Strategy

Throughout the election process, the candidate and his consultants constantly review the competition in an effort to determine how well their strategy is working. This point is well made by Kotler in the following quotation:

> The marketing control system is used to measure the ongoing results of a plan against the plan's goals and to take corrective action before it is too late. The corrective action may be to change the goals, plans, or implementation in the light of the new circumstances.[60]

Tactics were critical to the success of the Clinton organization, and Clinton himself understood what he had to do to win. According to Begala, Clinton controlled his message communicated in the media by spending large numbers of hours granting interviews and patiently answering any questions that were directed toward him. In particular, he consistently addressed the unrelenting questions that centered on the draft and his use of marijuana. But Clinton knew that voters wanted the election to be about their lives and not his. As a result, his messages emerged in a positive tone and focused on what he would do for voters and their children. On the other hand, Begala believed that Bush's message, including a constant bashing of Clinton's character, was negative. Part of Clinton's genius was his ability to project the same message at every campaign stop without giving the same rote speech. He accomplished this by talking directly with the voters, listening to what they had to say, and then integrating their concerns and stories into his speeches. According to Begala, this was as important as the focus groups.[61]

Conclusion

There is a strong reliance in modern-day campaigns on the use of information technology. Information technology is now used to a greater extent to shape the appeals that the candidates use to position themselves in the market. The information generated is then used to explain the attitudes and behaviors of the voters and to correspondingly alter the message and image of the candidate as he progresses through each stage of the political campaign. One measure of how well these tools work is to determine their predictive power. One of the tools discussed in this chapter is the poll. Whereas the poll is used by several of the power brokers, the predictions made by some of the major polling companies and television networks show how well they predicted in 1992.

According to the election results, Clinton actually received 42.9% of the vote, Bush 37.4%, and Perot 18.9%. When compared to several predictions made in the media, it looks as though the pollsters made very accurate calculations. The *Washington Post* most closely predicted the outcome for Clinton with 43%; Gallup and *ABC News* came in with the best prediction for Bush with 37%; and Harris had the best prediction of Perot with 17%. Prediction levels as precise as these afford a great deal of power. When these same polling techniques are used to identify voter attitudes and beliefs, they provide invaluable information to the candidate on how to shape his appeals to voter segments.[62]

This chapter concludes Part II of the book and ends the discussion of how the candidates were marketed in the 1992 election. I have detailed the way in which the candidates relied on sophisticated marketing strategies to get their message across to the American voters, and throughout the discussion of the techniques and tools used to influence this process, I have drawn similarities between the political and commercial marketplaces.

Clinton won the presidential race because he had the best marketing campaign. Not to minimize the significance of having a good product to work with, Clinton also campaigned as a strong leader and was able to convince voters of his leadership ability. He effectively communicated his message of change to the American electorate. Not only did Clinton have the discipline to stay with his message throughout the political campaign but by doing this he was able to refocus the debate from his character to the economy. His choice of Gore as his vice presidential running mate was a definite turning point in the campaign that gave the organization the momentum needed to win.

Through his successful use of market segmentation and positioning strategies, Clinton was able to win the nomination in the Democratic party. This accomplishment called for all of the skills that one would find in modern-day corporations, namely, competitiveness, flexibility, vision, and a willingness to rely on the most sophisticated marketing technologies. Perhaps more than any other single skill, Clinton's ability to market himself by talking about voters' concerns and desires rather than his own enabled the effective representation of his message. Clinton had a vision for America that voters bought into. This vision was well articulated on the sign that went up in the war room in Little Rock that said, "It's the Economy, Stupid."

Clinton's marketing strategy was very effective. His campaign platform incorporated the issues that voters were concerned about, especially the economy, jobs, and health care. These issues were likewise well communicated through the media. But most important, the Clinton organization was focused, organized, and run by a group of experts who understood the importance of marketing. They relied on focus groups and polls to direct their campaign strategy and were able to attract thousands of volunteers to help in their effort. Ultimately, Bill Clinton won because he developed a strategy that positioned him as a strong leader who advocated change.

Notes

1. McCarthy & Perreault (1991), p. 33.
2. *U.S. News and World Report* (1992, August 24), p. 22.
3. *U.S. News and World Report* (1992, January 27), p. 30.
4. *The New York Times* (1992, August 21).
5. Clinton/Gore campaign (1992).
6. *The New York Times* (1992, March 18).
7. *The New York Times* (1992, April 27).
8. *The New York Times* (1992, July 16).
9. *The New York Times* (1992, July 10).
10. *The New York Times* (1992, August 7).
11. Clinton/Gore campaign (1992).
12. *The New York Times* (1992, July 2).
13. *The New York Times* (1992, May 27).
14. *The New York Times* (1992, July 22).
15. *The New York Times* (1992, August 4).
16. *The New York Times* (1992, August 20).
17. *U.S. News and World Report* (1992, March 2), p. 31.
18. *The New York Times* (1992, October 22).
19. *The New York Times* (1992, October 3).
20. *The New York Times* (1992, October 5).
21. *The New York Times* (1992, August 26).
22. *The New York Times* (1992, June 15).
23. *The New York Times* (1992, July 16).
24. *The New York Times* (1992, July 16).
25. *The New York Times* (1992, April 3).
26. *The New York Times* (1992, August 19).
27. *The New York Times* (1992, September 21).
28. *The New York Times* (1992, August 21).
29. *The New York Times* (1992, September 10).
30. *The New York Times* (1992, October 5).
31. *The New York Times* (1992, October 20).
32. Clinton/Gore campaign (1992).
33. Clinton/Gore campaign (1992).

34. Clinton/Gore campaign (1992).
35. Clinton/Gore campaign (1992).
36. Clinton/Gore campaign (1992).
37. Cantril (1991), p. 139.
38. Cantril (1991), p. 134.
39. Asher (1992), p. 96.
40. Owen (1991), p. 94.
41. Bradburn & Sudman (1988), p. 225.
42. *The New York Times* (1992, May 7).
43. *The New York Times* (1992, June 9).
44. *U.S. News and World Report* (1992, July 27), p. 32.
45. *Time* (1992, September 21), p. 22.
46. *Time* (1992, September 21), p. 22.
47. *Time* (1992, September 21), p. 22.
48. *The New York Times* (1992, July 16).
49. *The New York Times* (1992, July 16).
50. *The New York Times* (1992, July 16).
51. *The New York Times* (1992, July 16).
52. *The New York Times* (1992, July 16).
53. *The New York Times* (1992, July 16).
54. *The New Yorker* (1992, October 12), p. 92.
55. *The New York Times* (1992, May 28).
56. *The New York Times* (1992, May 28).
57. *Time* (1992, July 13), p. 24.
58. *Time* (1992, July 13), p. 24.
59. *Time* (1992, July 13), p. 24.
60. Kotler (1982), p. 102.
61. Clinton/Gore campaign (1992).
62. *Marketing News* (1993, January 4), p. 13.

PART III

The Future of
Political Marketing

What changes can we expect in 1996? Will Larry King continue to be a key link between the candidates and the voters? Is a more direct link between candidates and voters healthy for the country? Is marketing helping or hurting the electoral process? Will Ross Perot or some other billionaire run a telemarketing campaign in 1996? If one does, what happens if he or she is successful and wins? What would it mean to have a president who has not gone through the usual checks and balances of the two-party system? These questions and more will be answered in the last section of this book.

There is no doubt that marketing will continue to play a vital role in the election process in this country and in other countries around the world. I have spelled out how a candidate is marketed to the voter in much the same way a product or a service is marketed to a consumer. Ethical issues that can be raised about the role of marketing in the commercial marketplace can equally be raised in the political market-place, which I will address in this last section. Finally, I have attempted to lay out in detail who the key power brokers are in politics today and how each one affects the other and the electoral system in general. I will also discuss the changing roles of the power brokers and examine the implication of these changes on the use of marketing in politics.

★7★

Dial-In Democracy

Nineteen ninety-two was an election year like never before seen in the United States. Former President George Bush referred to the political environment as being "weird." Indicative of this "weirdness," we saw the former vice president getting into a debate with a fictional TV character called Murphy Brown as well as Bill Clinton playing saxophone on *The Arsenio Hall Show*. We even had a news conference organized by a tabloid newspaper that was covered by a public affairs news station, C-Span, describing an alleged love affair between Clinton and Gennifer Flowers.

There was also Perot, a Texas billionaire and talk show guest who wanted to change the country and wound up changing his mind about running so many times that voters never knew if he was in or out. Of course, that did not stop him from continuing to appear on talk shows (which, by the way, continues now that we have already elected a new president). Then there was

Perot's running mate, James Stockdale, who confessed in the middle of the vice-presidential debate that he did not hear a question because his hearing aid was not turned up. Finally, at the end of the election, we heard an incumbent president calling his opponents "bozos."

Of particular interest in this election was the first real threat to our two-party system in many years. Perot received 19% of the popular vote, the best showing for an independent candidate in recent times. Perot's stunning showing was due in part to what was referred to earlier in the book as "dial-in democracy." The talk show format dominated the air waves, allowing candidates to circumvent the traditional media outlets. This created a direct link between the candidates and the voters in a way we had never seen before, which certainly was partially responsible for the increase in voter turnout in 1992.

Furthermore, few observers will forget the second debate in an electronic town hall setting (another first in 1992) when Bush could not respond to a question from an irate voter who demanded that Bush explain how the deficit had hurt him personally. Although the question did not really make any sense, Bush responded in a way that made him seem out of touch with the everyday lives of voters. In contrast, Clinton was at his best when he walked closer to the voter and gave a warm, sensitive answer. The voters acquired new power in this election.

Voters in the 1992 campaign became influential power brokers in the electoral process through their active participation and interaction with the media and the candidates. The talk show hosts became the conduits between the candidates and the voters. Clinton, long considered out of the race by most analysts and voters, rose to the challenge to win the race. An incumbent president, coming off a stunning victory over Iraq only a year earlier, was considered to be a shoo-in and lost.

James Carville's well-orchestrated campaign victory for Harris Wofford over Republican Dick Thornburgh, the former U.S. attorney general, spelled out the importance of the economy in this election. Wofford was a bureaucrat who had never run for statewide office but talked about health care reform and jobs, while Thornburgh emphasized his Washington clout and ties to Bush. Eventually, his connections to Bush wound up hurting his election chances. Bush's undoing was his failure to admit to the public that the country really was in a recession and that something had to be done about it. In addition, Bush played Clinton's avoidance of the draft for all it was worth only to find out that voters ultimately did not care. Still, he continued to press the point.

Change was the key theme in this election but not only in the candidates' appeals to voters. Change also permeated the very fabric of the electoral process and thus altered the way political campaigns are run. I have labeled the system responsible for this change "marketing." In an attempt to translate the impact of marketing on the electoral process, I drew analogies between business and politics, with the basic premise being that successful political campaigns today have the same consumer focus as successful businesses. This means that the political campaign begins and ends with the voter in mind.

The Changes in 1992

Technological Changes

Technological advances made in 1992 enabled presidential candidates to set up a more direct link with voters. At the same time, these advances gave voters what they have been yearning for throughout the campaign, namely, access to the candidates and a sense of empowerment. This year, for the first time, subscribers to Prodigy, a computer service network, have been able to take advantage of electronic database technology and access information about various aspects of the campaign. C-Span, a cable television station, followed the candidates around the nation to give viewers unedited insight into their activities.

New uses of old technologies were commonplace in this election. Television news programs incorporated the use of live focus groups at key junctures in the campaign to get insights into voters' thoughts and feelings about the candidates. They also used moment-to-moment tracking methods usually found in the research departments of advertising agencies to visually track voters' reactions to live broadcasts of candidates' speeches. ABC's *Nightline* program used this technology on one occasion, using colorful graphics on the television screen to trace the reactions of a sample of voters to parts of one of the debates. Clinton and Perot borrowed a business fixture, "satellite teleconferencing," to bring together simultaneously supporters in different states. As this technology advances, candidates and voters will be able to see one another simultaneously on a large screen.[1]

Looking ahead to the end of the 1990s, we will continue to see more technological advances. In particular, we see interactive television technology advancing very quickly. Along with the ability to tune in to over 500 different cable stations, consumers will soon have the ability to interact with their televisions. What will this mean to the candidate and the other power brokers? New technological advances will provide the gateway to more efficient methods of polling, promotion, and fund-raising. The technology will be used to support the movement toward more direct contact between the candidate and the voter.

As polling continues to play a more important role in the marketing of politicians, there has been a call for regulations. Self-regulation is one recommendation for intervention in the polling business with respect to the procedures that are followed in conducting a poll. Four ways of dealing with this issue have been advanced, including certification, the processing of complaints, peer review, and a set of stated principles. The American Association for Public Opinion Research is the professional forum that has in the past taken, and should in the future continue to take, the lead in this area.[2]

One last area that has had a tremendous impact on the electoral process is direct mail. The debate in direct mail is well framed in the following quotation:

> Given that direct marketing has both negative and positive effects on the American political system, what changes would help diminish the harms while maintaining the benefits? . . . One thing that can be done is to create stiff penalties for inaccurate mailings. Currently, by the time the FEC [Federal Election Commission] decides to take action, it is too late. A second remedy is to have all PACs [political action committees] send financial statements to their contributors.[3]

This area will continue to play a critical role in politics in the future and must be watched over carefully, especially in light of regulations in this area.

Changes in the Sociopolitical Makeup of the Electorate

There were several changes in the sociopolitical makeup of the electorate that had an impact on the election process in 1992. The population in this country is aging, and its concerns deal with issues of social security, health care, and the economy. As the elderly continue to grow in size as a voter segment, so will their influence on candidates. In fact, this segment will likely prove to be one of the decisive forces that shapes the campaign platforms of candidates in the next presidential election.

In addition, we now have a number of dual-income households in this country. As a result of this, the income differentials have created new classifications of the poor and of the affluent voter. The woman in the household has become more independent and is subsequently a stronger force in the electorate. Feminists and women's rights activists played an important role in this campaign. The growth in single-person households has likewise brought with it a set of new needs and demands on politicians, creating a new political reality for candidates. Many issues that benefit only families with children had to be reconsidered as the single-person household represented family households of a different kind.

The "Christian Right" spoke out loud and clear at the Republican convention and called for changes in family values in this country. Many critics and analysts pointed to the influence of the two Pats in the Republican party: Pat Robertson, who created a very influential political action committee that grew out of his run for the presidency in 1988; and Pat Buchanan, who gave a speech at the Republican convention that some believe dampened Bush's re-election chances. The Christian Right's call for family values and, in particular, their condemnation of gays and lesbians has sent a strong signal to voters that there will be divisions within not only the two-party system but also the Republican party. This will certainly have a tremendous impact on future Republican campaigns. The role of gays and lesbians in society and their ability to organize into a political force in the form of serious interest groups and political action committees will have to be dealt with by any candidate running in 1996. The issue of gays in the armed forces is one that will play itself out long before the 1996 election comes around. Clinton's embracing of this segment of voters definitely worked to his advantage in 1992.

Changes in Telecommunications

There were several changes in the telecommunications industry that played an important role in the 1992 election. Advertising on cable television was commonplace in this election. We will continue to see the candidates appear on shows like the *Home Shopping Network* and MTV. Cable stations afford candidates the opportunity to more carefully target their messages to viewers with special interests.

Voters took a more active role in this election than in the past several presidential elections. This level of participation came as a result of the advances made in the telecommunications industry. Jerry Brown, for example, was able to raise upward of $2 million using his toll-free telephone number as a means of connecting with the voter. But the real winner from the advances in this area was Perot, who received approximately 500,000 phone calls in a 24-hour period when he flashed his 800 number on *The Phil Donahue Show*. In order to accommodate the volume of phone calls, Perot had to use another 1,000 phone lines from the *Home Shopping Network*.[4]

In fact, when networks found out that it was good for business, talk show producers aggressively pursued the candidates in addition to the candidates pursuing them. Paula Zahn actually lobbied to get Bush onto her television program, *CBS This Morning*. Sam Donaldson lobbied to get Perot onto his program *Prime Time* but to no avail. Tamara Haddad, executive producer of the *Larry King Live* program, said that all of the networks were competing to be the first to get the candidates on their program.[5]

One issue that ties in to the popularity of the talk show format in politics is the fairness with which the interview is conducted. When Bush appeared on the *Larry King Live* show, a call was received from George Stephanopoulos, Clinton's communications director. The fairness of letting that call go through was questionable. Along with this new communications format must come some unwritten rules that prevent this kind of situation from happening in the future.

In some cases, when a candidate received an invitation from one program to make an appearance, he would take it to another program to get them to match it, thus increasing the candidate's exposure. Although the candidates would not admit this, some in the television industry argued that the shows with more seasoned and probably more aggressive interviewers were more likely to be the ones that the candidate avoided. However, this trend cannot be allowed to continue because the traditional media outlets play an important role in both an information dissemination capacity and an investigative capacity for voters.[6]

Structural Changes

There are some serious concerns about the primary and caucus system in this country, and questions continue to be raised about how and whether the system should be changed. The Super Tuesday primaries and caucuses in 11 different states the same day pose an enormous organizational challenge to the candidates. Candidates have to rely almost exclusively on the mass media to get their messages out to all of the states simultaneously, thus forcing candidates to rely even more heavily on telemarketing methods to win. Perot's difficulty in getting onto the ballot in all 50 states raises concerns about the fairness of the current rules and regulations.

There has been a blurring of the two major political parties and, as a result, there are candidates like Perot who made no claim to either of them. Does this mean that Americans will see a third party in this country in 1996? Perot's showing certainly gives him the ammunition to support congressional candidates who run in 1994 under the banner of a third party directed by him, which allows Perot to test the waters for another try at the presidency in 1996. Another issue that needs to be addressed is the cost of elections, where the money is coming from, and how much individuals and political action committees should be allowed to contribute to a candidate's organization. At the heart of campaign finance reform is the issue of converting the unlimited use of "soft" money (used by political parties to help candidates get elected) into "hard" money (which is regulated and limited).

There is talk in the Clinton administration of a trade-off of increased amounts of money that individuals can legally contribute if soft money is to be completely abolished. In a concerted effort to eliminate the continued influence of the rich and powerful contributors who now use the political parties as an alternative avenue to influence candidates, the Clinton administration has suggested one alternative solution: double the total amount individuals could contribute from the current level of $25,000 to $50,000, with half going to the candidate and half to the national party. Another proposal would be to triple the amount that individuals can currently contribute, up to $25,000 each for candidates, national parties, and state and local parties. Federal Election Commission records indicate that Clinton raised $29.8 million in soft money through the Democratic party in 1992. These contributions came from labor unions, corporations, and individuals. Clearly, soft money contributions will have to come from some other source if it is to be discontinued.[7]

Some of the changes that have been called for in the past with respect to the regulation of financial contributions include improvement of disclosures of political funds, elimination of loopholes around the current laws, use of government assistance only when necessary, and reinforcement of the political party's role to reduce the influence of political action committees. The need for these changes boils down to the fact that financial participation is next in importance to the actual vote of a citizen.[8]

Direct mail was to politics in the 1970s as telemarketing promises to be in the 1990s and beyond. Marketing technologies are powerful and have a strong impact on the electoral process. The polls are only the tip of the iceberg in this area. With access to voter lists in computer files that break down the electorate by every imaginable demographic and lifestyle characteristic, candidates have at their fingertips the opportunity to send political messages to voters that are so finely tuned voters will think the candidate is reading minds. Database marketing techniques, which allow candidates to more finely define their fund-raising appeals for money, will soon find their way into mainstream political advertising. We saw the first step in this direction with larger dollar amounts being spent in cable advertising, through which voter segments are more precisely targeted.

Changes in Voter Attitudes

Several issues crop up here, the first one of which is media sensationalism. The Gennifer Flowers interview will most likely limit the role of these stories in the future. Furthermore, Clinton's ability to deal with the story in addition to the sleazy way in which it was reported to the public will hopefully also discourage committing precious air time to stories that belong in the tabloids.

The voters said no to negative advertising this election year, however, some of the candidates still relied on it as a strategic tool. In particular, Bush's use of negative advertising in conjunction with the role of Vietnam brought up ill feelings. In all likelihood, this will not be an issue in 1996 and beyond, and Clinton's victory will most likely put an end to this potential hotbed in future elections. Still, there must be more accountability for the actions of all of the participants in the electoral process. In particular, the candidates have to take responsibility for the activities their campaign organizations engage in.

For the first time, and breaking a long-standing taboo, the candidates themselves attacked the media. Bush appeared in front of rallies with stickers that put down the media. Clinton also attacked the media for their unfair coverage of his private life. The whole structure of reporting the news is changing in this country, with local newscasts assuming a greater role in disseminating information to voters. These changes have heightened voters' awareness of the increased power of the media.

Voters seemed to like the shift in the media to a more interactive approach to reporting the news. The 1992 campaign was waged on the talk shows not the evening news. Although this interaction is healthy from a participatory perspective, it throws a tremendous amount of power into the hands of talk show hosts such as Larry King or Phil Donahue and away from newscasters such as Sam Donaldson and Dan Rather. In the future networks will likely realize that they must adapt to this new political format and will begin to put their best interviewers on programs that allow for more interaction with voters.

As the political campaign process changes in this country, so have voter attitudes about how we should deal with it. One approach is well described by Sabato, who states the following:

> Voters' cynicism about politics leads them to believe any charge of corruption or moral turpitude against a politician. The public is often as unwilling as the press to view candidates in a balanced way. To remedy this situation, the schools must take the lead, stressing from kindergarten through college the study of current events, American government, and political history. A better informed citizenry will more easily evaluate and select media outlets, and care more about issue and substance and less about sensationalism.[9]

Along this line of thinking, it would be healthy to see more education about the role of marketing in political campaigns in high school classes and even in political science courses in colleges.

Implications for 1996

The Impact of Ross Perot's Candidacy

Perot's candidacy was responsible for several changes, some of which were very positive and others of which were not. Among the positive developments was that he introduced the political world to the use of infomercials, a 30- or more minute commercial that is meant to be both informative and persuasive. In addition, he ran a nontraditional campaign using television and in particular talk shows as the channels through which he connected with voters. The talk show format is healthy but should not necessarily replace the traditional television interview formats in which the questioning is more in-depth. It is good, on the one hand, to see the candidates in a more natural setting, where interviews are less confrontational, but at the same time it is healthy to see how the candidates respond to the pressure that comes with the more traditional interviews voters are more familiar with in this country.

What was not beneficial to the system was the way in which Perot manip-
ulated the media. By using a confrontational approach with the media and
attacking the campaign process, Perot escaped the kind of scrutiny that there
should have been for an "unknown" candidate. Perhaps he used confronta-
tion to avoid the tough questions. We in this country should never come this
close to letting someone get to the top in the polls without having a clear idea
about who the person is and what he stands for. But in July Perot was number
one in the polls, and most people only knew that he stood for change but had
no idea about how he would solve the country's problems. Some analysts
believe that Perot might have won the election had he not dropped out of the
race.

Perot completely eclipsed the other third-party candidates who every 4
years try to win votes. He received about 19% of the popular vote in one of
the biggest turnouts in modern history and collected 20% in 28 states. Prior
to Perot's campaign, the best showing for a third-party candidate was by Robert
LaFollette in 1924. Perot's advantage in the election was his wealth, but
another advantage was that he realized he did not need the traditional media.
In effect, Perot turned talk shows into the whistle stops of the campaign.

In the end, television derailed Perot's bid, particularly when he appeared
on *60 Minutes* and said that he dropped out of the race in the summer because
he believed the Republican party planned to sabotage his campaign. The alleged
plans included bugging his business telephones, disrupting his daughter's
wedding, and publishing altered, provocative photographs of her. As many
had expected, Republican officials, including Bush, called the accusations
nonsense.

Was it the end or just the beginning? Many are saying that the forces
unleashed by Perot's candidacy are not going away. In fact, some three months
after the election, voters still saw Perot as well as his 800 number on interview
programs, asking people to pay $15 to join his United We Stand organization.
In effect, he is building a direct mailing list that he may use to solicit funds
and support from whomever he chooses. Perhaps the best indicator of a
discontented electorate was the voter turnout, which was up for the first time
since 1972, and the voters' willingness to vote for a third-party candidate.

If Clinton fails to put the economy back on track, the probability of an
emerging third party may increase. If Clinton succeeds, he will have molded
a new coalition; if not, we will certainly see Perot with a third party supporting
him. Third-party challenges have always depended on charismatic leadership
at the top, which Perot certainly could provide. The fact that people want

accountability in Washington, and the fact that voter dissatisfaction will stay high as long as Perot keeps a high profile, makes a third party a real possibility in this country.

Is the ability of candidates like Perot to enter the race by using a telemarketing campaign healthy for society? On the one hand, it is healthy because it represents an extreme example of free speech in this country. At the same time, it is frightening that a candidate can run a telemarketing campaign that entirely circumvents the traditional political processes that have been built into our system and make such a strong showing.

How could an independent like Perot get along with a Congress that operates on the two-party system? This was one issue that was not raised seriously in 1992 and must be addressed in 1996 if Perot is to be a contender again. Evidence of Perot's continued influence came prior to Clinton's State of the Union address, when Clinton was reported in the news to have conferred with Perot about the details of his speech. In the final assessment, Perot revitalized the TV infomercial so that it served a purpose for products beyond cures for balding. Ultimately, his legacy exists in his work with the media, where he helped make Larry King a star of the 1992 election.

How Will Marketing Be Used?

If Clinton's tenure is only a one-term presidency, it will be an open door to Perot or someone else in Perot's position to take advantage of a new political technology already in place as a result of the 1992 election. Candidates are being marketed, and the sooner we all realize and understand how it is happening, the sooner we can begin to work to make sure that marketing is used in a way that helps strengthen the political process in this country.

One lesson that Clinton brought with him from his campaign is that marketing can be used not only to run for office but to run the country. Even after a month into his presidency, Clinton still seemed to be campaigning, taking his message directly to the people by relying on the same methods he used during the race. His economic program was promoted to the American public over cable television and in electronic town hall meetings. However, this activity came at the expense of fewer press conferences than many would have liked.

Clinton used a satellite hookup to 2,500 communities early on in his presidency to make a pitch for his economics package, which was stalled in the Senate. This was part of his effort to build up grass-roots support for his plan and was also reminiscent of the war room–like atmosphere that drove his campaign. What we see happening is Clinton using marketing as a way of governing the country. Along with his satellite hookup came a campaign to call over 1 million voters and to send out over 500,000 pieces of mail to build support for his program. The same people who ran his campaign, now in various posts in his administration, ran this operation.[10]

Instead of targeting states, Clinton now targets key lobbyists who are influential with Congress. As they successfully did every morning at their convention, the Democratic National Committee (headed up by Clinton's former campaign chair) sent out faxes to supporters giving them talking points in support of Clinton's program. Clinton hoped to reach some of the more moderate Republicans as well as moderate and conservative Democrats through this effort. There is word that Celia Fischer, who worked under Carville during the campaign, will head up the lobbying effort to market Hillary Clinton's health care program from a nonprofit operation.[11]

If Perot chooses, he has the ammunition to wage a fierce campaign in 1996. He has the name recognition, the leadership potential, the grass-roots manpower, the money, and, most important, a message grows stronger if the economy worsens. Why would Perot want to run if Clinton is still popular in 1996? He would need to keep his following intact for a more serious run in 2000. Perot is in a win-win situation wearing his "outsider" hat because he currently represents the only viable option to voters still disgruntled with politics as usual. Although he does not belong to either of the two major parties, this will turn out to be to his advantage because the only real benefits of belonging to one are the financial and grass-roots support that come along with it. Through his political action committee, Perot will receive all of the grass-roots support he needs.

From the Republican side, there will be a tremendous amount of infighting to win over the heart of the party, especially among Jack Kemp, Dan Quayle, Phil Gramm, Pat Buchanan, and other leaders of various wings of the party. Some say that for the Republicans to win they have to clean the house of the religious right. In a sense, the Republicans will find themselves on the same side of the fence the Democrats found themselves on in 1992. If the economy is flourishing by 1995, then Clinton is sure to be a hard one to beat, barring any scandal or unforseen circumstances. However, if the economy does not respond to the program Clinton ran on, he has got trouble. Clinton will not have the luxury of saying that Congress did not allow him to get his program through because the majority rule now lies with the Democrats in Congress.

A weak economy could also serve to bring some of the Democrats who did not run in 1992 back into the fold in 1996. This includes Bill Bradley, Sam Nunn, Mario Cuomo, and others. But the economy would have to be very weak for this to happen. In addition, there will be Hillary Clinton to look for in 1996. Many will measure her accomplishments as closely as they examine her husband's. Many are wondering whether Hillary will let her role as first lady change her or whether she will change the role as it is defined. Some media have suggested that we should look beyond 1996 to the year 2000 when Hillary Clinton possibly changes seats with her husband and runs for the White House herself.

The new political campaign technology described in this book will be intact in 1996, however, in a more interactive form than it is in now. Talk shows and electronic town meetings have set the stage for a more involved voter whose appetite for active participation in the process will in all likelihood get stronger in the next presidential campaign. Advanced telecommunication technology will establish interactive capabilities that will allow candidates to hold town hall meetings with television viewers across the country. Cable television will become a two-way channel of communication.

Certainly, one of the key voter segments in 1996 is going to be the voters who supported Perot, namely, the astounding 19% of the electorate (if not more by 1996) that all of the candidates know they will need to win. If Perot's campaign approach is any indication of what these voters like, we can be sure to see the candidates going direct to the voters in 1996. We can also expect to see these voters and their leader, Perot, repudiate again the use of negative advertising.

A code of ethics needs to be developed that addresses the responsibilities of the power brokers involved in the process. This means the media, the candidates, the consultants, the political action committees and interest groups that represent the voters, the pollsters, the media, and the political parties must take on more responsibility in their influential roles. There must be the elimination of the "win at all costs" attitude among power brokers. CBS and NBC aired segments of newscasts during the course of the 1992 campaign that looked at the candidates to see if they were telling the truth; these were referred to by various names, with the one on CBS called a "Reality Check." This is the kind of reporting and responsible action on the part of one power broker, the media, that needs to be carried out more vigorously by all involved.

Conclusion

Let us look back to what happened in 1992 and try to understand how marketing has influenced the electoral process in this country. I have outlined and analyzed the evolution of marketing in politics and where we stand today with respect to who controls the process. The forces in the environment that influence the marketing and political campaigns have been identified and will certainly continue to play a role in the shaping of politics in the future. Two people showed the American electorate in this campaign that an understanding of how marketing and politics intersect can result in both influencing the outcome and winning an election. Clinton played by new rules in politics and won, while Perot changed the rules for winning in the future. Perot proved that voters are interested in more than images and look to candidates to supply them with hard facts about the issues. The voter came out of this election more powerful than ever. The outpouring of voters on election day was proof of the sense of empowerment that they felt in this election. Perot continues to influence the political process by acting in a watchdog capacity to make sure that Clinton lives up to his promises.

Since the election in November 1992, Perot has been aggressively in pursuit of new members for his organization, United We Stand. He asks voters for a $15 membership fee and claims the fee gives the voter a sense of empowerment and an active role in his or her pursuits. However, any marketing professional knows it is a very effective way of developing a direct mail list that can be tapped into for a whole host of activities, including asking members to write their representatives in Washington and to donate time and money, or using this grass-roots foundation to wage a bid for the White House in 1996.

One of Perot's postelection activities was his national referendum, that is, his 17-point questionnaire that set the agenda for his political action committee. *TV Guide* carried the ballot in its March 20, 1993, edition. Perot wrote to every newspaper editor in the country and asked that the referendum questionnaire be published for free to give those who did not watch the television program an opportunity to participate. We have yet to see how the results of this survey will be used, but, according to Perot, he plans to circulate the results to every level of government in the country to let the officials know what the people are thinking. The poll continues to be used as a powerful instrument in election campaigns. The use of 900 number polls are troublesome. Although there is always a disclaimer that these are not random polls and do not reflect the thinking of the whole population, it is not likely that every potential voter who hears the results of this kind of poll truly understands that disclaimer. Whoever is contracting for the poll is doing a disservice to the political process in this country when information is erroneously presented.

The polls drove the media coverage of the 1992 campaign. Newspaper reporters, television journalists, and the media in general reported and conducted more polls in this election than ever before. As long as the polls (and the horse race mentality that they breed) do not supersede the coverage of issues and events, it is a healthy activity for our political process. However, the people suffer when the poll becomes the focal point in the media and serves as the dominant influence in the reporting of the election. Winning and losing is a major part of the American psyche and, when it becomes the focus of an election, we too easily forget about what matters most, namely, leadership and the issues.

The media as power brokers continue to play an increasingly important role in politics. Their scrutiny of the candidates running for president in 1992 ran the gamut from excellent investigative reporting to tabloid journalism. A new low in the coverage of politics was reached when several networks covered the Gennifer Flowers press conference. To the extent that the issue of a candidate's character is at stake in the reporting of events, the media should continue to be aggressive in their pursuit of the truth. However, when television ratings are the driving force behind decisions to pursue stories about a candidate's sex life, the media will only destroy the trust that they need to maintain their credibility.

Furthermore, the players in the media who have historically been entrusted the role of interviewing the candidates changed in 1992. Thanks to Clinton's use of electronic town meetings, there was a significant shift in power from the investigative-style reporting of reporters like Sam Donaldson to talk show–style interviews of hosts like Larry King. Along with that shift came the increased status and power of cable television and a diminishing role for networks in reporting election news. Voters in 1992 had a yearning for more interaction with the candidates, and they received the opportunity for it. However, voters still need to hear the tough questions from interviewers like Ted Koppel. These questions lead to "high-pressure" situations that elicit answers that give voters tremendous insight into the leadership capabilities and ideas of the candidates. For the benefit of voters, there must be a mix of both types of journalism.

Programs like C-Span received more attention from viewers in 1992 than in 1988 because of the appetite of voters to get more insight into the activities of the candidates. Coverage of a candidate's speech, for example, would start from the time he would step down off the airplane, to the ride into town, to the handshaking between candidate and voters after the speech. Similarly, talk shows and appearances on television shows that in 1988 would have been unheard of, such as Clinton's appearance on MTV and *The Arsenio Hall Show*, became commonplace events. To the extent that the disenfranchised voter, who would not otherwise participate in the political process, gets involved, the country stands to gain from candidate appearances like this.

There is a call by many to go back to the days when candidates would rise up through the traditional ranks of the party to become the nominee for president (a process that is still largely followed at local and state levels). But this is not likely to happen because of the structural changes that have taken place over the last two decades. As long as the power brokers that have taken over some of the activities of the party can be trusted to operate in a moral and ethical way, our political process has the potential to be strengthened. Political action committees, interest groups, and the media, for example, can play a very significant role in empowering the voter and increasing their levels of participation in the political process.

Structural shifts that have taken place over the past two decades in the United States have altered the political campaign process and put more pressure on candidates to rely on consultants for winning elections. For example, the primary process places the candidate in a position where he must have a well-organized team to be able to formulate and implement strategy quickly. Media experts, pollsters, and campaign strategists implement some of the most sophisticated marketing innovations to craft candidate images and segment markets.

The candidate has no choice but to rely on consultants to know what message to target to his audience. For example, Super Tuesday does not afford the candidate much opportunity to travel to 11 different states in a single day, and therefore satellite teleconferencing must be relied on to get the candidate onto the evening news in all of these states, with selected messages targeted to voters with different concerns. Candidates need to segment their markets, position themselves, and choose appropriate strategies to win office in this day and age.

The financial regulations have changed dramatically since the Campaign Reform Acts were enacted. These changes have pressured candidates to hire direct mail specialists and fund-raisers to help them drum up the money to proceed from one primary campaign to another. All of these consultants have changed the way political campaigns are run; they have taken over the reins of control from the party bosses.

The political campaign process was altered by Clinton and Perot in 1992 and will continue to be altered by critical opinion leaders in the years to come. Is this healthy? The answer depends on the level of integrity brought into the electoral process by the power brokers shaping politics in this country. For example, if consultants rely on negative and misleading tactics to get candidates into office, our political process suffers. If candidates get into office on the basis of images crafted around promises that are not kept when the politician starts to govern, the nation suffers.

Marketing made the difference between winning and losing in the 1992 presidential election. I have shown how marketing was used by Clinton as a campaign strategy to win the White House. The verdict is out on whether the goals underlying Clinton's marketing campaign were pursued with integrity—We will have to wait to see whether he delivers on his promises. I believe marketing can be used as a tool in a constructive manner if it follows the marketing concept, which presupposes that there is an implicit service contract between the candidate and the voter. Clinton continues to use the same marketing tools to bolster public support for his programs. As long as marketing is used to shape public opinion in an open and honest way, the political process will be strengthened from the transformation described here.

Notes

1. *The New York Times* (1992, June 9).
2. Cantril, A. H. (1991), p. 175.
3. Godwin, R. K. (1988), p. 151.
4. *Time* (1992, April 6), p. 26.
5. *The New York Times* (1992, July 6).
6. *The New York Times* (1992, July 6).
7. *USA Today* (1993, March 26).
8. Alexander, H. E. (1992), p. 161.
9. Sabato, L. (1991), p. 245.
10. *Chicago Sun Times* (1993, April 14).
11. *Chicago Sun Times* (1993, April 14).

References

Abramson, J. B., Arterton, F. C., & Orren, G. R. (1988). *The electronic commonwealth: The impact of new media technologies on democratic politics.* New York: Basic Books.

Alexander, H. E. (1992). *Financing politics: Money, elections, and political reform.* Washington, DC: Congressional Quarterly Press.

Asher, H. (1992). *Polling and the public: What every citizen should know.* Washington, DC: Congressional Quarterly Press.

Bradburn, M., & Sudman, S. (1988). *Polls and surveys: Understanding what they tell us.* San Francisco: Jossey-Bass.

Cantril, A. H. (1991). *The opinion connection: Polling, politics, and the press.* Washington, DC: Congressional Quarterly Press.

Clinton, B. C., & Gore, A. (1992). *Putting people first.* New York: Times Books.

Clinton/Gore campaign: Post election news conference (1992, November 4). TBS, C-Span.

Cook, R. (1992). *Race for the presidency: Winning the 1992 nomination.* Washington, DC: Congressional Quarterly Press.

Drucker, P. F. (1986). *The frontiers of management.* New York: Truman Talley.

Euchner, C. C., & Maltese, J. A. (1992). *Selecting the president: From Washington to Bush.* Washington, DC: Congressional Quarterly.

Godwin, R. K. (1988). *One billion dollars of influence: The direct marketing of politics.* Chatham, NJ: Chatham House.

Jamieson, K. H. (1992). *Packaging the presidency: A history and criticism of presidential campaign advertising.* New York: Oxford University Press.

Johnson, R. M. (1971). Market segmentation: A strategic management tool. *Journal of Marketing Research, 8*, 13-18.

Kotler, P. (1982). *Marketing for nonprofit organizations.* Englewood Cliffs, NJ: Prentice Hall.

Kraus, S. (1990). *Mass communication and political information processing.* Hillsdale, NJ: Lawrence Erlbaum.

Luntz, F. I. (1988). *Candidates, consultants & campaigns: The style and substance of American electioneering.* New York: Blackwell.

McCarthy, E. J., & Perreault, W. D., Jr. (1991). *Essentials of marketing.* Homewood, IL: Irwin.

McCombs, M., Einsiedel, E., & Weaver, D. (1991). *Contemporary public opinion: Issues and the news.* Hillsdale, NJ: Lawrence Erlbaum.

McCubbins, M. D. (Ed.). (1992). *Under the watchful eye.* Washington, DC: Congressional Quarterly Press.

McGinniss, J. (1969). *The selling of the president.* New York: Trident.

Newman, B. I., & Sheth, J. N. (1985). *Political marketing: Readings and annotated bibliography.* Chicago, IL: American Marketing Association.

Newman, B. I., & Sheth, J. N. (1987). *A theory of political choice behavior.* New York: Praeger.

Nimmo, D. (1974). Images and voters' decision-making processes. *Advances in Consumer Research, 1*, 771-781.

Owen, D. (1991). *Media messages in American presidential elections.* New York: Greenwood.

Perot, R. (1992). *United we stand.* New York: Hyperion.

Pika, J. A., Mosley, Z., & Watson, R. A. (1992). *The presidential contest: With a guide to the 1992 presidential race.* Washington, DC: Congressional Quarterly Press.

Polsby, N. W. (1980). *Presidential elections: Contemporary strategies of American electoral politics.* New York: Free Press.

Pomper, G. M. (1988). *Voters, elections and parties: The practice of democratic theory.* New Brunswick, NJ: Transaction.

Pool, I. D., & Abelson, R. (1961). The Simulmatics project. *Public Opinion Quarterly, 25*, 167-183.

Sabato, L. J. (1991). *Feeding frenzy.* New York: Free Press.

Shani, D., & Chalasani, S. (1992). Exploiting niches using relationship marketing. *Journal of Consumer Marketing, 9*(3), 33-42.

Sheth, J. N., Newman, B. I., & Gross, B. L. (1991). *Consumption values and market choices: Theory and applications.* Cincinnati, OH: South-Western Publishing.

White, T. H. (1960). *The making of the president.* New York: Antheneum House.

White, T. H. (1982). *America in search of itself: The making of the president 1956-1980.* New York: Harper & Row.

Author Index

Subject Index

About the Author

Bruce I. Newman is an Associate Professor of Marketing in the Kellstadt Graduate School of Business, DePaul University. Prior to that, he was on the faculty of Baruch College, City University of New York, and the University of Wisconsin-Milwaukee. He was also a visiting professor at Trinity College in Dublin, Ireland, and a visiting scholar at F.M.D. Research Institute in Oslo, Norway. He received his B.S., M.B.A., and Ph.D. in marketing from the University of Illinois in Champaign-Urbana.

Dr. Newman has published extensively and is internationally known for his contributions in the fields of political marketing, voting behavior, and consumer behavior. His coedited book (with Jagdish N. Sheth) *Political Marketing: Readings and Annotated Bibliography* is the first and only formal integration of the literature in political marketing. He has coauthored two books, *Consumption Values and Market Choices* (with Jagdish N. Sheth and Barbara Gross) and *A Theory of Political Choice Behavior* (with Jagdish N. Sheth). Both books put forward an innovative theory of choice behavior that has been extensively applied to both voters and consumers.

Dr. Newman recently received the *Ehrenring* (Ring of Honor) from the Austrian Advertising Research Association in Vienna for his widespread research in political marketing. He is the first American recipient of this award in the 30 years it has been awarded.